BILLY GRAHAM
Evangelistic Associatio
Always Good News.

Dear Friend,

I am pleased to send you this copy of *Great Is His Faithfulness: Stories of God-Inspired Crusade Hymns*. This book includes essays written by my father and musicians with the Billy Graham Evangelistic Association Crusade team.

Great Is His Faithfulness tells the stories behind some of our favorite hymns—and includes practical application of the lyrics to our everyday lives. Each chapter also concludes with a prayer that focuses on God's truth in that hymn. It is my prayer that you will be blessed and encouraged as you read about these classic hymns and that you will be inspired to "*sing to the Lord a new song, for he has done marvelous things*" (Psalm 98:1, NIV).

For more than 60 years, the Billy Graham Evangelistic Association has worked to take the Good News of Jesus Christ throughout the world by every effective means available, and I'm excited about what God will do in the years ahead.

We would appreciate knowing how our ministry has touched your life. May God richly bless you.

Sincerely,

Franklin Graham
President

If you would like to know more about our ministry, please contact us:

IN THE U.S.:
Billy Graham Evangelistic Association
1 Billy Graham Parkway
Charlotte, NC 28201-0001
BillyGraham.org
info@bgea.org
Toll-free: 1-877-247-2426

IN CANADA:
Billy Graham Evangelistic
  Association of Canada
20 Hopewell Way NE
Calgary, AB T3J 5H5
BillyGraham.ca
Toll-free: 1-888-393-0003

BILLY GRAHAM
EVANGELISTIC ASSOCIATION

Great Is
HIS
Faithfulness

STORIES OF GOD-INSPIRED CRUSADE HYMNS

BILLY
GRAHAM
Evangelistic Association

Always Good News.

Charlotte, North Carolina

This *Billy Graham Library Selection* is published by
the Billy Graham Evangelistic Association.

ISBN: 978-1-59328-374-2

Contents

Preface

I love to hear the great choirs sing at our Crusades around the world—often in languages I cannot understand—but God can. I love the Gospel songs of George Beverly Shea and the other soloists on our team who travel with us. I love the final verse in the Psalms (the greatest hymn collection of all time) that tells us, "Let everything that has breath praise the Lord."

God put a song into us, but sin garbled it, distorted it, and brought discord into our lives. When a person repents and puts his or her trust unreservedly in Jesus Christ, God gives back the melody that was almost muted. That is the secret of the Christian life.

Cliff Barrows and Don Hustad, two team musicians who have been my close associates, have made a priceless gift to the church by writing and compiling this volume of hymn stories. Not many people know that the greatest Christian hymns and songs have often come out of the deep wells of life: wells of adversity, of suffering, of tragedy. It is inspiring to know that when events have turned dark and somber, these men and women have been able to tune their souls to a pitch unheard apart from the mind of Christ. The result has been a multiplied blessing to all humankind.

"Is any among you merry?" asked the Apostle James. "Let him sing psalms" (cf. James 5:13). "*Be filled with the Spirit,*" wrote the Apostle Paul, "*speaking to yourselves in psalms and hymns and spiritual songs, singing and making melody in your heart to the Lord; giving thanks always for all things unto God and the Father in the name of our Lord Jesus Christ*" (Ephesians 5:18–20, KJV).

I unreservedly commend this book. May God bless you as you read of what He can do through the power of music; and may you join the mighty choir of the faithful by lifting your own voice in heartfelt praise to the King of kings and Lord of lords who loved us and gave Himself for us.

Billy Graham, 1967

Foreword

One of the greatest contributions to the spiritual development of my life has come from the influence of sacred songs. As a young boy I learned to love our Gospel songs and hymns, as well as the Bible, at my mother's knee.

We of the Billy Graham team have witnessed the lasting appeal of hymns and their power to unite the hearts of a congregation. Wherever Christians gather, the singing of hymns and songs has been a vital and meaningful part of worship.

The stories behind the hymns have always fascinated me. I believe they provide some of our most inspiring devotional literature. This book brings together some of the favorites of Billy Graham, and of the members of our music staff. Of course, not all our favorites—or yours—are here, but there are enough to give you a hymn a day for a month to study, to memorize, to make your very own.

Try using them for your personal worship or for family devotions. We believe you will find that one of the purposes of this book—to help you sing "with the spirit and with the understanding also"—is being fulfilled.

In writing the stories, there has been an honest attempt to present the facts concerning the hymns, their origins, and their significance in the Billy Graham Crusades as we have known them. We do not claim that these are all the facts. Wherever we have erred or omitted something others may deem important, we ask indulgence.

I am indebted to all the members of the team who have shared their favorite hymn stories along with their personal experiences and observations. Lee Fisher, a gifted musician and Bible scholar, who has been an intimate friend and associate of Dr. Graham, gave invaluable help in checking the manuscripts.

A special word of thanks goes to my beloved colleague, Don Hustad, whose fellowship and musicianship was a great source of inspiration to me. His unique gifts and abilities have well qualified him for the task of research and writing which he untiringly pursued. If the song of the Lord resounds more assuredly from your heart and life as a result of this little volume, all of the time and effort put into it will be worthwhile.

Yours, in the glad song our Savior brings,
Cliff Barrows, 1967

Great Is Thy Faithfulness

Thomas Obediah Chisholm, 1923   William Marion Runyan, 1923

1. Great is Thy faith-ful-ness, O God my Fa-ther, there is no
2. Sum-mer and win-ter, and spring-time and har-vest, sun, moon and
3. Par-don for sin and a peace that en-dur-eth, Thy own dear

shad-ow of turn-ing with Thee; Thou chang-est not, Thy com-
stars in their cours-es a-bove join with all na-ture in
pres-ence to cheer and to guide; strength for to-day and bright

pas-sions they fail not; as Thou hast been Thou for-ev-er wilt be.
man-i-fold wit-ness to Thy great faith-ful-ness, mer-cy and love.
hope for to-mor-row, bless-ings all mine, with ten thou-sand be-side!

Refrain

Great is Thy faith-ful-ness! Great is Thy faith-ful-ness! Morn-ing by

morn-ing new mer-cies I see; all I have need-ed Thy

hand hath pro-vid-ed; great is Thy faith-ful-ness, Lord un-to me!

Great Is Thy Faithfulness
Hymn story by George Beverly Shea

One of God's men who most influenced my life was Dr. Will H. Houghton, the late president of Moody Bible Institute. In 1938 when I was working in an insurance office in New York City and seeking to know what God wanted me to do with my life, Dr. Houghton asked me if I would like to come to Chicago and sing on the Institute's radio station, WMBI. One of our programs was *Hymns From the Chapel*—fifteen minutes of hymns at the early hour of 8:15 every morning. Along about 1942, Don Hustad joined me on the program, playing the organ.

I learned afterward that the program was often heard in those days by a young man named Billy Graham who was attending Wheaton College, just west of Chicago. A short time later, Billy asked me to help him in a broadcast from the Village Church in Western Springs where he was student pastor; this association led to our work together in the evangelistic Crusades. How I thank God for His faithfulness in leading me one step at a time into His plan for my life!

Looking back, I remember also Dr. Houghton's tall, dark, commanding presence as he led Moody's chapel services with a wonderful combination of dignity, humor, and song. He loved hymns and especially appreciated the song "Great Is Thy Faithfulness." Its music had been composed by William M. Runyan, who often appeared in person at the Institute in those days. Mr. Runyan later said that it was Dr. Houghton's frequent use of the hymn which helped it to become popular with the general public.

It would be wrong to assume that every hymn has been written or has become well known as the result of some dramatic experience. Some authors have simply made it a habit to write poems regularly, perhaps one every day. Out of the hundreds that flow from the pen, only a few will be worthy of publishing.

Thomas Chisholm, a Methodist life insurance agent, gave us these inspiring words. He says that there were no special circumstances surrounding their writing. He simply penned the lines from his impressions about God's faithfulness as told in the Bible and sent them, with several other poems, to his friend and collaborator William Runyan.

Our team had the privilege of introducing "Great Is Thy Faithfulness" to audiences in Great Britain in 1954, and the song became a favorite there, too. It has often been sung at British wedding services and was included in hymn books.

The opening stanza and refrain are taken directly from scriptural affirmations about God. "*His compassions fail not. They are new every morning: great is thy faithfulness*" (Lamentations 3:22–23, KJV). "*Every good gift and every perfect gift is from above, and comes down from the Father of lights, with whom there is no variation or shadow of turning*" (James 1:17). In other words, God is always like the bright sunlight characteristic of midday; there is never a shadow to cloud His complete and perfect faithfulness.

God's faithfulness derives from another attribute of His character—His immutability. This is our answer to a few so-called theologians who have proclaimed that "God is dead." He is alive! He is eternal! He cannot change by so much as a shadow!

In many ways nature shows us that God is faithful. Every sunset is followed by a sunrise. Every winter is followed by a summer. Whenever we plant seed, we can count on a harvest. In the sky we see innumerable stars all moving in patterns which can be charted by astronomers thousands of years in advance.

But even more clearly, through His dealings with mortal men and women, we have learned that God is faithful. He has promised in His Word to forgive our sins and to give us peace of mind and heart; when we accept Christ His Son as our Lord and Savior, He fulfills His pledge. Morning by morning, day after day, we feel His presence in our hearts. Surely we can look forward with hope to His presence, even at the end of life's journey.

I am often reassured by these words of an unknown believer: "Fear not tomorrow, for God is already there!"

Prayer for the Day:

Thank You, Lord, that You have shown Your faithfulness throughout all generations. The unchanging patterns of the seasons, plants, and stars all give us assurance that You do not change. As I begin each day in Your presence, give me that enduring peace that You promise to those who trust in You.

Amazing Grace

John Newton, 1779 (verses 1-4)
John Rees, ca. 1859 (verse 5)

Early American folk hymn, 19th c.;
harm. Edwin Othello Excell, 1900

1. A - maz - ing grace how sweet the sound that
2. 'Twas grace that taught my heart to fear, and
3. The Lord has pro - mised good to me, His
4. Through man - y dan - gers, toils, and snares, I
5. When we've been there ten thous - and years, bright

saved a wretch like me! I once was lost, but
grace my fears re - lieved; how pre - cious did that
Word my hope se - cures; He will my shield and
have al - read - y come; 'tis grace hath brought me
shin - ing as the sun; we've no less days to

now am found; was blind, but now I see.
grace ap - pear, the hour I first be - lieved.
por - tion be, as long as life en - dures.
safe thus far, and grace will lead me home.
sing God's praise than when we've first be - gun.

Amazing Grace
Hymn story by Billy Graham

One Sunday during the Earls Court Crusade in London in 1966, we were driving between speaking engagements in the university towns of Oxford and Cambridge. Suddenly I noticed that we were passing through the village of Olney, and I remarked to my wife, "There's a famous church and graveyard here. Let's stop to visit them."

Riding through the Olney village square, we passed the former home of William Cowper. It had been converted to a museum housing the personal effects of that great English poet, to whom we are indebted for classic poetry as well as for some of our finest hymns. This village is also famous as the place where the Shrove Tuesday pancake races originated.

The Olney parish church of Saints Peter and Paul was built in the fourteenth century, but much of the original beauty and dignity remains. In the corner of the churchyard, almost overgrown with tall grass, we found what we were looking for—a large tombstone with these words inscribed:

> John Newton, Clerk; once an infidel and libertine, a servant of slaves in Africa, was by the rich mercy of our Lord and Savior Jesus Christ preserved, restored, pardoned, and appointed to preach the faith he had long labored to destroy.

Newton was the son of a sea captain who was engaged in the Mediterranean trade. His mother died when he was six, and after only two years of formal schooling he joined his father's ship at the age of eleven. His early life was one of immorality, debauchery, and failure. He was rejected by his father, in trouble with all his employers, and finally jailed and degraded. In later years he served on slave ships, where he so incurred the hatred of his employer's black wife that he became virtually a "slave of slaves."

This miserable seaman was brought to his senses by reading Thomas à Kempis's book *Imitation of Christ*. His actual conversion was the result of a violent storm in which he almost lost his life. At the age of thirty-nine, John Newton became a minister and gave the rest of his life to serving God in the church. During the fifteen years he was the pastor at Olney, he wrote many hymns. Together with William Cowper, he published a hymnal which was widely used.

It seems to me that "Amazing Grace" is really Newton's own testimony of his conversion and of his life as a Christian. He might have begun the hymn with the first stanza of another of his poems, "He Died for Me," but these words have somehow dropped out of use:

> In evil long I took delight,
> Unawed by shame or fear,
> Till a new object struck my sight,
> And stopped my wild career.

"God's grace" has been defined as "His undeserved favor." It was this grace that reached out to John Newton. When he learned that Christ loved him and had died for him, he was amazed. It was this grace which made him conscious that he was a sinner ("grace taught my heart to fear") and then assured him that his sins were forgiven ("grace my fears relieved"). So it is with all of us. We are all "great sinners" not only because of transgressions committed, but also because we fall short of God's standard for our lives. And this "amazing grace" is available to all of us.

As Christian believers we continue to experience God's undeserved love and favor throughout all of life. Every day He forgives our shortcomings, if we confess them. Every day He supplies all our needs.

John Newton never ceased to marvel at God's mercy and grace that had been granted to him. Over the mantelpiece in the Olney vicarage he had placed an inscription which still remains:

> *Since thou wast precious in my sight, thou hast been honourable* (Isaiah 43:4, KJV). *But thou shalt remember that thou wast a bondman in the land of Egypt, and the Lord thy God redeemed thee* (Deuteronomy 15:15, KJV).

He never forgot the sea. Late in life, when he was pastor of St. Mary Woolnoth in London, Newton entered the pulpit in the uniform of a sailor, with a Bible in one hand and a hymnbook in the other. His mind was failing then, and he sometimes had to be reminded what he was preaching about. When someone suggested that he should retire, he replied, "What, shall the old African blasphemer stop while he can speak?" On another occasion, he said, "My memory is nearly gone, but I remember two things: that I am a great sinner, and that Christ is a great Savior."

They tell us that the last stanza of this song was not written by John Newton. But I think he would agree that it is a fitting climax to his testimony. After he and we have been in heaven for ten thousand years worshiping our Lord, we will still have endless time to sing of His amazing grace!

Prayer for the Day:

Dear God, I am amazed and grateful for Your grace, extended to someone as undeserving as I am. Give me the strength to share Your love and grace with people I know, as Newton did, for as long as I can still speak. Forgive my shortcomings today and lead me until You take me home.

When I Survey the Wondrous Cross

Isaac Watts, 1707

Gregorian chant,
arr. Lowell Mason, 1824

1. When I sur - vey the won - drous cross on which the Prince of Glo - ry died, my rich - est gain I count but loss, and pour con - tempt on all my pride.

2. For - bid it, Lord, that I should boast, save in the death of Christ, my God; all the vain things that charm me most, I sac - ri - fice them to His blood.

3. See, from His head, His hands, His feet, sor - row and love flow min - gled down. Did e'er such love and sor - row meet, or thorns com - pose so rich a crown?

4. Were the whole realm of na - ture mine, that were a pres - ent far too small; love so a - maz - ing, so di - vine, de - mands my soul, my life, my all.

When I Survey the Wondrous Cross
Hymn story by Tedd Smith

One of the most important names among English hymn writers is that of Isaac Watts. Born into a merchant's home in Southampton in 1674, Watts was sickly and rather unattractive as a child. At the same time, by today's standards he was very precocious. Young Isaac began to study Latin at the age of four, and added Greek when he was nine, French at eleven, and Hebrew at thirteen!

Watts was also interested in poetry, and it is said that much of his boyish talk came out in rhyme and meter. His father soon tired of conversation of this nature and outlawed the poetic improvising. But Isaac was irrepressible, and to enforce this prohibition, his father resorted to a spanking. Through his tears the boy cried:

> O father, do some pity take,
> And I will no more verses make.

When he was fifteen, the young poet turned his talents to the service of the church. At that time, Christians in England sang nothing but strict and rather stilted versions of the Old Testament psalms, introduced line after line by a precentor and repeated line after line by the congregation. Said Watts: "The singing of God's praise is the part of worship nighest heaven, and its performance among us is the worst on earth." Whereupon his father, a leading deacon in the Congregational church, charged him: "Young man, give us something better!"

Isaac Watts accepted the challenge and launched an avocation which earned him the title "the father of English hymnody." As a Congregationalist minister he wrote over six hundred hymns, including the magnificent "When I Survey the Wondrous Cross."

Throughout the years this hymn has been acclaimed. It was ranked as "one of the four which stand at the head of all hymns in the English language" by John Julian, our greatest hymnologist. Many people would agree that it is the *very best* English hymn, a claim made by the nineteenth-century literary critic Matthew Arnold.

In Crusade services and in concerts, I have often played two tunes which have been associated with these words. The tune "Hamburg" is best known in America and was written in 1824 by one of our own important musicians, Lowell Mason, when he was living in Savannah, Georgia. This simple yet solemn melody uses only five notes and is based on an ancient Gregorian "tone" or scale. I also enjoy playing the tune "Rockingham," which we sang more often in British Crusades. This tune was published in 1790 by Edward Miller; its actual composer is not known. I believe that these two melodies bring out the different meanings of the words of the hymn's stanzas.

It seems to me that Isaac Watts wrote this text as if he were standing at the foot of Christ's cross, together with the disciple John, the faithful women, Jesus' mother, the Roman soldiers, and the excited, shouting mob. When I play or sing the hymn, I try to make Watts's ideas and words my own. With him, I cannot help but marvel at the incredulity of the scene—the "Prince of glory" nailed to a tree by sinful men. Jesus, dying for me! For it was my sins which He bore on that terrible day. Therefore, my voice was one of those which had cried, in Pilate's court, "Crucify Him!" My hand—as well as the hand of the Roman soldier—had wielded the hammer which drove the nails into His body.

Then, in my mind's eye, I see the blood which flowed from His wounds, showing—as the hymn suggests—His sorrow because of my sins and also His great love for me. How can I fail to say, *"God forbid that I should boast except in the cross of our Lord Jesus Christ, by whom the world has been crucified to me, and I to the world"* (Galatians 6:14)? It is difficult to understand the latter part of this Scripture verse, but Watts explains it in the last stanza of his hymn. Our Lord does not want me to try to repay Him for His love and His sacrifice with my own sorrow, my good works, or with my material things. If I owned the "whole realm of nature," it wouldn't be enough to give Him in return. Christ wants *more* than this! He wants me—"my soul, my life, my all."

When you read this hymn, I hope that you will make the words and their meaning your very own, as I have done.

Prayer for the Day:

Forgive me, Lord, for the times when pride tempts me to think that my efforts or my possessions are significant. Allow me to sense the meaning of Your amazing love and to acknowledge my own role in Your suffering. Because of Your great love, I surrender my soul, my life, my all.

Love Divine, All Loves Excelling

Charles Wesley, 1747

John Zundel, 1870

1. Love di-vine, all loves ex-cel-ling, joy of heaven, to earth come down;
2. Breathe, O breathe Thy lov-ing Spir-it in-to ev-ery trou-bled breast!
3. Come, Al-might-y to de-liv-er, let us all Thy life re-ceive;
4. Fin-ish, then, Thy new cre-a-tion; pure and spot-less let us be.

fix in us Thy hum-ble dwell-ing; all Thy faith-ful mer-cies crown!
Let us all in Thee in-her-it; let us find that sec-ond rest.
sud-den-ly re-turn and nev-er, nev-er-more Thy tem-ples leave.
Let us see Thy great sal-va-tion per-fect-ly re-stored in Thee;

Je-sus, Thou art all com-pas-sion, pure, un-bound-ed love Thou art;
Take a-way our bent to sin-ning; *Al-pha and O-me-ga* be;
Thee we would be al-ways bless-ing, serve Thee as Thy hosts a-bove,
changed from glo-ry in-to glo-ry, till in heaven we take our place,

vis-it us with Thy sal-va-tion; en-ter ev-ery trem-bling heart.
end of faith, as its be-gin-ning, set our hearts at lib-er-ty.
pray and praise Thee with-out ceas-ing, glo-ry in Thy per-fect love.
till we cast our crowns be-fore Thee, lost in won-der, love, and praise.

Love Divine, All Loves Excelling
Hymn story by Cliff Barrows

All of us have experienced the "lift" that comes with singing a great hymn together. Uniting our hearts and voices in Christian song gives us a sense of release over our fears and weaknesses.

This has been my experience over and over again. One of the instances which is still vivid to me happened in 1961, during the Manchester, England, Crusade. Just as the meetings were about to start, Billy Graham became quite seriously ill. Leighton Ford was called to be his substitute for the first week of Crusade services.

Billy had been scheduled to speak to the ministers of London just before the Crusade opened. You can imagine my feelings when he sent word that I should represent him and speak at that meeting. The British pastors were themselves thorough scholars and often brilliant preachers. And they were expecting to hear Billy Graham, not me!

At the beginning of that meeting in Westminster's Central Hall, the ministers joined in singing this great hymn of Charles Wesley. Most of these British clergymen were also well acquainted with hymn texts and hymn tunes, and they sang gloriously. Accompanied by the grand piano and the great pipe organ and using the Welsh tune "Blaenwern," these familiar words lifted our hearts in praise and prayer to God. I felt God's strength evident through the singing; He blessed our meeting together, despite my fears and their disappointment.

This is perhaps one of our most familiar hymns, and yet I fear that most Americans have only a vague notion of what it says. Reading only the title or the first line, we assume that it is a hymn extolling the love of God. But its message is far more specific than that.

Who is the "Joy of heaven, to earth come down"? It is Jesus Christ who comes to make our hearts His humble dwelling. The third line of the first stanza makes it clear. Jesus is "pure, unbounded love"—the love of God made manifest—the love of God incarnate, in the flesh. The hymn, then, is really a prayer to Christ who is Love Divine.

But there are still other obscure phrases in the hymn. What is "that second rest" that we are asking to find? Here it helps to know something of the doctrinal emphasis of the Wesleys and of all the early Methodists. They believed that after conversion there is a second experience for the Christian—that when one totally consecrates himself to Christ, his heart is cleansed from all sin. The experience is called "entire sanctification." They believe that an individual who is sanctified—"made holy"—experiences a relief from the struggle with sin in his life and finds a new "rest" or liberty in Christ. This is the "second rest" mentioned in the hymn, and it is derived from Hebrews 4:9, *"There remains therefore a rest for the people of God."* This also helps us understand the "Alpha and Omega" phrase in the second stanza. The two experiences of conversion and sanctification are thought of as the *"beginning* of faith" and the *"end* of faith."

We must admit that there are differences among Christians with regard to this doctrine of sanctification. But there is common agreement that when we reach the end of ourselves and yield our bodies and minds completely to God, we do find spiritual power and freedom that we cannot otherwise know. Many Christians of varied church backgrounds have witnessed that for them this was a single crisis experience that came after they first knew Jesus Christ as Savior. Others would say that their act of consecration was repeated daily, and that, for them, "becoming holy" was a matter of progress and growth.

Of course, for all Christians, any experience should be only the beginning of Christian maturing, of "growing in grace." We must all be changed "from glory to glory"—knowing more about Christ and becoming more like Him, until we "take our place in heaven."

And, let us not be afraid of the expression "Christian holiness." Actually it means more than freedom from sin—this is a negative concept that only partly explains the phrase. "Holiness" is really "wholeness"—a balanced personality that possesses all virtues and strengths, in body, mind and spirit. Spiritual "wholeness" or maturity is something we should all desire and seek.

Prayer for the Day:

Jesus, I want to know You more and become more like You every day. Give me Your Spirit so that I may live a life of holiness and wholeness. Dwell in me and remove any sinful desires so that I can serve You and worship You with my body, mind, and soul.

I Surrender All

Judson Wheeler Van DeVenter, 1896

Winfield Scott Weeden, 1896

1. All to Je-sus I sur-ren-der, all to Him I free-ly give;
2. All to Je-sus I sur-ren-der, hum-bly at His feet I bow,
3. All to Je-sus I sur-ren-der, make me, Sav-ior, whol-ly Thine;
4. All to Je-sus I sur-ren-der, Lord, I give my-self to Thee;

I will ev-er love and trust Him, in His pres-ence dai-ly live.
world-ly plea-sures all for-sak-en, take me, Je-sus, take me now.
may Thy Ho-ly Spir-it fill me, may I know Thy power di-vine.
fill me with Thy love and pow-er, let Thy bless-ing fall on me.

Refrain

I sur-ren-der all, I sur-ren-der all.
I sur-ren-der all, I sur-ren-der all.

All to Thee, my bless-ed Sav-ior, I sur-ren-der all.

I Surrender All
Hymn story by Billy Graham

One of the evangelists who influenced my early preaching was also a hymnnist who wrote "I Surrender All"—the Rev. Mr. J.W. Van DeVenter. He was a regular visitor at the Florida Bible Institute (later renamed Trinity College of Florida) in the late 1930s. We students loved this kind, deeply spiritual gentleman and often gathered in his winter home at Tampa, Florida, for an evening of fellowship and singing.

Mr. Van DeVenter was not always a minister. According to his own testimony, his first interest and passion was for art. Having finished college, he taught school for a while in order to finance his continued study of drawing and painting. Later he became supervisor of art in the public schools of Sharon, Pennsylvania.

At that time, evangelistic meetings were being held in his church, and Van DeVenter became involved in counseling and personal work. Since he had obvious ability in this direction, several of his friends urged him to give up teaching and become an evangelist. For five years he wavered between this challenge and his ambition to become a recognized artist.

As he told the story himself:

> At last the pivotal hour of my life came and I surrendered all. A new day was ushered into my life. I became an evangelist and discovered down deep in my soul a talent hitherto unknown to me. God had hidden a song in my heart, and touching a tender chord He caused me to sing songs I had never sung before.

The hymn "I Surrender All" was written some time later in his life, when J.W. Van DeVenter recalled this long struggle and final yielding to God's will.

We begin to surrender to God when we first accept Jesus Christ as Savior and Lord. The word *Lord* means just that—"Master." At the close of a Crusade meeting, I would ask those who came forward to pray, using these words: "I receive Christ as Savior; I accept Him as Lord." It is a mistake to think that we can receive Christ's offer of forgiveness and then go out to live our lives as we please. From that moment of commitment, God has a claim on us and we must expect Him to tell us how we should live.

Often this truth comes to an individual in a more forceful way, a little later in his Christian life and walk. A young person may be considering whom to marry or what profession to pursue. A man or woman may be contemplating a new business relationship or weighing obligations to the church, to the community, to family. Suddenly the true meaning of what the Bible says dawns on them: "*Your body is the temple of the Holy Spirit, who lives in you, and ... you are not the owner of your own body ... You have been bought, and at what a price! Therefore bring glory to God both in your body and your spirit, for they both belong to him*" (1 Corinthians 6:19–20, Phillips).

We should never fear to give God complete control over our lives. He loves us more than we love ourselves, and He will only plan what is best for us. It isn't always true, as it was with Reverend Van DeVenter, that God takes us down a different path from that which we would naturally follow. But if He does, we may be sure that it will be a happier and more fruitful life than the one we would have planned for ourselves.

Nor is it true that a person who yields up his own will becomes a weakling—a "namby-pamby milquetoast." Just the opposite is true. When we surrender our all to God, we find that we live with a new confidence, a new strength of purpose. No longer do we worry about the decisions we make, for now God is making them; from here on, He is responsible for the outcome. Furthermore, we find that He gives us His own supernatural strength to meet the challenge of each day!

Prayer for the Day:

Thank You, God, for loving me. Lead me in Your paths of righteousness. Show me what Your plan is for my life, and help me to meet the challenges of each day, with Your strength and courage.

In the Garden

Charles Austin Miles, 1912

Charles Austin Miles, 1912

In the Garden
Hymn story by Don Hustad

Changing trends in church music was the discussion topic at a dinner party I attended several years ago on a seminary campus. The wife of a theology professor complained that song leaders and choir directors seem to ignore many favorite hymns, such as "In the Garden."

"You don't sing the old favorites that we learned as youngsters," she said. "I've even heard some church musicians criticize 'In the Garden' as sentimental and meaningless."

I couldn't resist the temptation. "What garden?" I asked.

"What difference does it make 'what garden?'" she retorted, with just a little heat.

The truth is, it makes quite a lot of difference. If the hymn is just a childhood favorite with pleasant phrases about gardens and birds and roses, it cannot be really meaningful in a vital worship experience today. This kind of an attachment for a song is a superficial emotion which is a good example of what we call sentimentality.

But it doesn't have to be that way. There was a garden, and the hymn can be meaningful! C. Austin Miles, the composer, gives us the clue himself:

> One day in March, 1912, I was seated in the darkroom where I kept my photographic equipment and organ. I drew my Bible toward me; it opened at my favorite chapter, John 20. ... That meeting of Jesus and Mary had lost none of its power to charm. As I read it that day, I seemed to be part of the scene. I became a silent witness to that dramatic moment in Mary's life when she knelt before her Lord, and cried, 'Rabboni!' ... Under the inspiration of this vision I wrote as quickly as the words could be formed the poem exactly as it has since appeared. That same evening I wrote the music. (From *Forty Gospel Hymn Stories* by George W. Sanville)

The specific reference to a garden becomes much clearer when we learn that C. Austin Miles was writing about the first Easter morning and the garden in which Jesus was buried. It was here Mary Magdalene came alone very early, "while the dew was still on the roses." When Jesus first spoke to her, she thought it was the gardener; but when He called her by name, she recognized His voice.

It is difficult to imagine what Mary's feelings and actions were at that moment. She had seen Jesus die on the cross. She was now coming to anoint His dead body with spices. But there He was, standing before her and talking to her. He was alive! She may have been startled at first, but when His identity became clear, she was filled with joy—as the song says, like a melody ringing in her heart! No doubt Mary wanted nothing more than to stay there in the garden with Jesus, but He ordered her to go and tell His disciples what had happened.

Mary's experience is relived by every person who confronts the risen Christ and realizes His presence in the routine of daily life. We too can "walk and talk" with Christ and be assured that we belong to Him. This experience is very real to a believer and brings a joy that is beyond any other satisfaction. Indeed, it may sometimes seem that no one else has ever known as much delight as we experience, walking each day with Christ. At least, this was author Miles' conviction when he wrote: "The joy we share as we tarry there, none other has ever known."

When we take time to know Christ intimately through prayer and meditation, we too may feel that we want to stay in His presence forever. But He "bids us go" as He did Mary, to tell others of His death, His resurrection and ascension, and His promise of coming again. His command to go is, in a sense, a "voice of woe" because people must be warned to turn from their sins if they are to escape God's judgment. And we are the only messengers God has to take this news to the world. As Paul the apostle said: "*Woe is me if I do not preach the gospel!*" (1 Corinthians 9:16).

"In the Garden" was a favorite song during the days Homer Rodeheaver led singing for the Billy Sunday campaigns. It can be just as significant today if we remember its true meaning as we sing.

Prayer for the Day:

Jesus, spending time with You is a sweet delight. I want to know You more and stay in Your presence. Yet You have commanded me to go and tell others the Good News. Thank You for walking alongside me as I share Your love with someone today.

Just As I Am

Charlotte Elliott, 1834

William Batchelder Bradbury, ca. 1849

1. Just as I am, with-out one plea, but that Thy
2. Just as I am, and wait-ing not to rid my
3. Just as I am, though tossed a-bout with man-y a
4. Just as I am, poor, wretch-ed, blind; sight, rich-es,
5. Just as I am, Thou wilt re-ceive, wilt wel-come,
6. Just as I am, Thy love un-known hath bro-ken

blood was shed for me, and that Thou biddest me
soul of one dark blot, to Thee whose blood can
con-flict, man-y a doubt, fight-ings with-in and
heal-ing of the mind, yea, all I need in
par-don, cleanse, re-lieve, be-cause Thy prom-ise
ev-ery bar-rier down; now to be Thine, yea,

come to Thee, O Lamb of God, I come! I come!
cleanse each spot, O Lamb of God, I come! I come!
fears with-out, O Lamb of God, I come! I come!
Thee to find, O Lamb of God, I come! I come!
I be-lieve, O Lamb of God, I come! I come!
Thine a-lone, O Lamb of God, I come! I come!

Just As I Am
Hymn story by Billy Graham

When I was converted in 1937 under the ministry of the evangelist Mordecai Ham, two invitation songs were used and a total of eight stanzas were sung. I did not respond to the invitation until the final verse of the second song, and I have always been grateful that the evangelist waited so patiently. One of these hymns was "Just As I Am, Without One Plea."

We used this hymn in almost every one of our Crusades. Some critics objected to singing at the time of the invitation because they claimed it has an excessive emotional impact on the audience. But on the occasions when we used no music at all, others complained about the "impressive, dramatic silence" that is broken only by the footsteps of those who are coming forward.

There are several reasons why we chose the hymn "Just As I Am" for use at this most important moment in a Crusade service. For one thing, it rings with a strong, positive note. Other songs give Christ's invitation just as clearly, but this one keeps repeating the affirmative response, "O Lamb of God, I come." The choir would sing it while the people were walking down the long aisle or across the turf of an outdoor stadium, and the hymn verbalized just what each of them was doing.

This song also presents the strongest possible biblical basis for the call of Christ. It repeats many of the reasons a person should respond when the Spirit of God speaks to him. The first stanza, like most great hymns, has captured the truth of the entire hymn. We should feel free to come to God because He has invited us to come, and because Jesus died on the cross in order to reconcile us to His Father.

Everyone who comes into the world—whether in Christian or pagan, civilized or primitive cultures—has the same innate awareness of God. They want to approach God and to be accepted by Him. The book of Genesis tells us that Cain, son of Adam, came to God with an offering of fruit and grain produced through his own hard work, but God did not recognize him. His brother Abel's approach to worship was with the sacrifice of an animal, as God had decreed; he was welcomed and accepted by God.

Today as well, people cannot apparently give up the idea that God will accept them because they "are good and decent" or because they have done good works for others or for the church. But the Bible says that we have "no plea" before God—no claim on His love or His forgiveness—except that Jesus Christ shed His blood for us. God accepts the sacrifice made by His own sinless Son.

In coming to Christ we should not wait until we have straightened out our lives a bit. No small improvement we can effect will make us any more acceptable to Him. God loves us just as we are, and we should come that way.

We should also come to Christ because He alone can solve the problems of our lives. Only He can free us from our sense of guilt and from our mental frustrations and anguish. Only He can pardon and cleanse us, in order to make us presentable before God.

We should come to Christ even though we don't understand all about salvation. I believe that God has designed His offer so it is necessary to take a final leap of faith to bridge the gulf of things we cannot comprehend. It is interesting to learn that Charlotte Elliott, author of this hymn, was an invalid during much of her life and that these words were written to express her victory over spiritual doubt.

The year was 1834 and Miss Elliott was living in Brighton in her native England. She was forty-five years old and had been a devoted Christian for many years. Even so, she was plagued with unhappiness because of her seeming uselessness, for everyone around her was busy in the service of God. In her extreme depression she was tempted to doubt the reality of her spiritual life.

Gathering strength and resolve, Charlotte Elliott deliberately wrote down the reasons for her trust in Christ. This hymn was the result. In the ensuing years, countless Christians have shared her experience and renewed their faith over and over through these familiar words.

When I come to present my credentials at the gate of heaven, it will mean nothing that I have traveled around the world preaching the Gospel. Then, as when I was first converted, I will say:

Just as I am, without one plea,
But that Thy blood was shed for me,
And that Thou biddest me come to Thee,
O Lamb of God, I come.

Prayer for the Day:

It is not in my power, God, but Yours that I can enter Your kingdom. Cleanse me from the stains of my past mistakes and give me the ability to live a life that pleases You. Thank You for accepting me just as I am.

Guide Me, O Thou Great Jehovah

William Williams, 1745; tr. Peter Williams, 1771

John Hughes, 1907

1. Guide me, O Thou great Je - ho - vah, pil - grim through this bar - ren land.
2. O - pen now the crys - tal foun-tain, whence the heal - ing stream doth flow;
3. When I tread the verge of Jor - dan, bid my anx - ious fears sub - side;

I am weak, but Thou art might - y; hold me with Thy power - ful hand.
let the fire and cloud - y pil - lar lead me all my jour - ney through.
death of death and hell's de - struc-tion, land me safe on Ca - naan's side.

Bread of Heav - en, Bread of Heav - en, feed me till I want no
Strong De - liv - erer, Strong De - liv - erer, be Thou still my strength and
Songs of prais - es, songs of prais - es, I will ev - er give to

more; (want no more;) feed me till I want no more.
shield; (strength and shield;) be Thou still my strength and shield.
Thee; (give to Thee;) I will ev - er give to Thee.

Guide Me, O Thou Great Jehovah

Hymn story by Don Hustad

The Welsh people may well be the most enthusiastic singers in the world. Their centuries-old tradition, that everybody loves to sing, has been perpetuated in the International Eisteddfod, which is held at Llangollen each year.

The Welsh miners customarily sang on their way to work in the coal pits. In the great spiritual revivals which have come to Wales several times during the past two hundred years, music was often more important than preaching. Their pastors and evangelists were never disturbed if the sermon was interrupted by a spontaneous outburst of congregational song. For it was often through singing that the Spirit of God moved the congregation to repentance and faith in Christ.

One of Wales's greatest hymn writers in the late eighteenth century was the layman-preacher William Williams. During forty years of ministry he traveled almost 100,000 miles, on foot and on horseback, preaching and singing. The best known of his eight hundred hymns is "Guide Me, O Thou Great Jehovah."

During a choir concert I conducted in Cardiff in 1954, we invited the congregation to join us in singing this hymn. After we had finished the stanzas we knew in English, someone in the audience led in the Welsh version. On and on they sang, hymn after hymn, until we were almost unable to finish the choral program.

Today, as in much of the world, people in Wales do not attend church as faithfully as they once did. But you will still hear them sing this hymn—just as we sing our national anthem—at the beginning of rugby matches!

From the words of the first line, we understand that this is a prayer for God's care and guidance throughout life. It recalls incidents from the forty-year journey of Israel through the desert, after they had left Egypt for their trek to the promised land of Canaan. Although they were delayed in reaching their new home because of sin and unbelief, God continued to lead them and to provide for their needs each day of those forty years.

We too are pilgrims in a journey from the cradle to the grave, and many times our lives will seem like a "barren land," a wilderness. Many times in our weakness we call upon the mighty God to sustain us with His powerful hand. As He fed the children of Israel each day with manna—a supernatural "bread from heaven"—so He has promised to "supply our every need" (cf. Philippians 4:19). We are nourished by the Word of God, which another hymn calls the "bread of life"; and it is God's written Word which tells of the "Word made flesh," Jesus Christ.

Twice during the Hebrews' years of wandering, they became faint because they had no water. At the command of God, Moses struck a large rock with his wooden staff, and out of it flowed a pure, crystalline stream which saved their lives. The Apostle Paul once told the story and drew the same spiritual lesson as the hymn presents:

> *All ate the same spiritual food, and all drank the same spiritual drink. For they drank of that spiritual Rock that followed them, and that Rock was Christ.* (1 Corinthians 10:3–4)

God supplied the basic physical needs of the Hebrews. He also led them miraculously, day by day and step by step. During the day they followed a cloud which moved before the marching column; at night, the cloud appeared to be a "pillar of fire" which hung over the camp to remind them that God was there, watching over them. Even so, the Christian believer today may experience God's guidance in all the little things, as well as in the major decisions of life.

When the ancient Jewish pilgrims finally reached the Jordan River which formed the boundary of the promised Canaan, there, too, God was with them. Joshua 3:14–17 tells us that when the people moved forward in faith, the river parted so that they could walk over on dry ground. At the end of our life's journey, death may appear to be a river we dread to cross. But when Christ is our Lord, He walks with us through the waters of death and leads us with great happiness to the other side—our Canaan, our eternal home.

One of the joys of the Christian life is the consciousness that God is with us each moment, guiding, protecting, and providing. This is why we love to sing, with our brothers and sisters in Wales:

> Songs of praises, songs of praises,
> I will ever give to Thee.

Prayer for the Day:

When I am weak, Lord, or when I am in need, I know that I can trust You to hold me and to lead me, as You did the Israelites in the wilderness. Feed me daily with Your words of life.

How Great Thou Art!

Carl Boberg, 1886;
tr. and adapt. Stuart K. Hine, 1953

Traditional Swedish folk tune,
adapt. Stuart K. Hine, 1953

1. O Lord, my God, when I in awe-some won-der con-sid-er
2. When through the woods and for-est glades I wan-der and hear the
3. And when I think that God, His Son not spar-ing, sent Him to
4. When Christ shall come with shout of ac - cla - ma - tion and take me

all the worlds Thy hands have made; I see the stars, I hear the roll-ing
birds sing sweet-ly in the trees; when I look down from loft-y moun-tain
die, I scarce can take it in, that on the cross, my bur-den glad-ly
home, what joy shall fill my heart! Then I shall bow in hum-ble ad-or-

thun-der, Thy power through-out the u - ni-verse dis-played.
gran-deur, and hear the brook and feel the gen-tle breeze.
bear-ing, He bled and died to take a - way my sin.
a - tion, and there pro - claim, "My God, how great Thou art!"

Refrain

Then sings my soul, my Sav-ior God, to Thee, "How great Thou

art,   how great Thou art!" Then sings my soul, my Sav-ior God, to

Thee,   "How great Thou art,   how great Thou art!"

How Great Thou Art!
Hymn story by George Beverly Shea

During the London Crusade at Harringay Arena in 1954, my friend Mr. Andrew Gray, of the publishing firm Pickering and Inglis, Ltd., handed me a little four-page leaflet containing a "new hymn." We receive many contributions of this kind, and at first I did not examine it closely. But I did notice that it had words in both English and Russian, and that it had a very strong and worshipful title, "How Great Thou Art!"

A few weeks later I learned that this "new hymn" by S. K. Hine was the final result of almost seventy years of literary activity, involving several different writers and translators. It had first been written in Sweden in 1885 or 1886 by Rev. Carl Boberg, a well-known preacher and religious editor, who also served for fifteen years as a senator in the Swedish parliament. The original title was "O Store Gud" (O Great God).

An earlier translation into English was published in 1925 under the title "O Mighty God," but it never really caught on. "How Great Thou Art!" arrived in America by a much more devious route!

The German version "Wie gross bist Du" had been translated from the original Swedish by Manfred von Glehn, a resident of Estonia, in 1907. Five years later, in 1912, the Rev. Ivan S. Prokhanov—known as the "Martin Luther of modern Russia"—published the hymn in St. Petersburg in his own language, probably translating it from von Glehn's German poem. It was included in a booklet entitled *Cymbals*—"a collection of spiritual songs translated from various languages." The interesting title was derived from Psalm 150:5, "*Praise him upon the loud cymbals: praise him upon the high sounding cymbals*" (KJV).

In 1922, several of Prokhanov's hymn-booklets, including *Cymbals*, were combined in a large volume, *The Songs of a Christian*. It was published (in Russian) in New York City, by Prokhanov's friends of the American Bible Society. Finally, in 1927, this larger book was reprinted in Russia, again through the assistance of Prokhanov's American supporters. This new release of Russian evangelical hymns brought "How Great Thou Art!" to the attention of an English missionary couple, Mr. and Mrs. Stuart K. Hine, and it was widely used by them in evangelism in the western Ukraine. After singing it for many years in Russian, Mr. Hine translated three verses into English. When the Second World War broke out, the Hines returned to Britain, where the fourth stanza was added in 1948.

The completed song was printed in 1949 in a Russian Gospel magazine published by Mr. Hine. Reprints were requested by missionaries all over the world, and it was one of those leaflets that was given to us in 1954. We first sang "How Great Thou Art!" in the Toronto, Canada, Crusade of 1955. Cliff Barrows and his large volunteer choir assisted in the majestic refrains. Soon after, we used it on *The Hour of Decision* and in American Crusades. In the New York meetings of 1957, the choir joined me in singing it ninety-nine times! It became a keynote of praise each evening.

Reading the first verses of this song of worship, we think of the opening words of Psalm 19: "*The heavens declare the glory of God and the firmament shows His handiwork.*" Carl Boberg once said that the inspiration for his original hymn was the beauty of the Swedish meadows and lakes after a summer thunderstorm.

Stuart Hine also wrote that the first verse of his English version came to life after a memorable thunderstorm in a Carpathian mountain village in Czechoslovakia, where he had to seek shelter for the night. On a later occasion, he visited the mountain country of Bukovina in Romania, and in the grandeur of the "woods and forest glades" heard a group of young Christians burst instinctively into song, accompanied by their mandolins and guitars. The hymn they sang was "How Great Thou Art!" with Prokhanov's Russian text, and it was this experience which moved Hine to pen his second stanza.

Yes, God talks to us through His creation—the heavens and the earth declare His glory. But the greatness of God is shown even more completely in the salvation He has planned and provided for us. What wisdom it reveals! What love it discloses! As the third stanza confesses, this greatness is more than I can understand: "I scarce can take it in."

Mr. Hine also said that his final verse was written just after the Second World War, when many refugees from Eastern Europe were streaming into England. Although they had found greater safety and freedom in their adopted land, their incessant question was "When are we going home?" It is only when we reach our heavenly home that we will fully comprehend the greatness of our God. As the Apostle Paul reminds us: "*Now we see things imperfectly, like puzzling reflections in a mirror, but then we will see everything with perfect clarity. All that I know now is partial and incomplete, but then I will know everything completely, just as God now knows me completely*" (1 Corinthians 13:12, NLT). In that day we shall "bow in humble adoration" and say, "My God, how great Thou art!"

Prayer for the Day:

Dear God, I am awed by the ways You used different individuals and different languages to bring this inspiring hymn to people around the world. Help me not to take Your awesome creation for granted. I look forward with great anticipation to the day when I can proclaim Your greatness before Your throne. In the meantime, I praise You with my entire being.

Blessed Assurance

Fanny Jane Crosby, 1873

Phoebe Palmer Knapp, 1873

1. Bless-ed as - sur - ance, Je-sus is mine! Oh, what a fore-taste of
2. Per - fect sub-mis - sion, per-fect de-light, vi-sions of rap - ture now
3. Per - fect sub-mis - sion, all is at rest, I in my Sav - ior am

glo - ry di - vine! Heir of sal - va - tion, pur-chase of God,
burst on my sight: an - gels de - scend - ing bring from a - bove
hap-py and blest: Watch-ing and wait - ing, look-ing a - bove,

Refrain

born of His Spir - it, washed in His blood.
ech - oes of mer - cy, whis-pers of love. This is my sto - ry, this is my
filled with His good-ness, lost in His love.

song, prais-ing my Sav - ior all the day long; this is my sto - ry,

this is my song, prais-ing my Sav - ior all the day long.

Blessed Assurance
Hymn story by Cliff Barrows

Several years ago I stood in a cemetery at Bridgeport, Connecticut, and looked at an unpretentious gravestone marked "Aunt Fanny." I recalled the life of a remarkable woman blind almost from birth who was probably the most important Gospel song writer of the last century and a half. How many people have been won to faith in Christ by the hymns of Fanny Crosby!

One of Miss Crosby's close friends was Mrs. Joseph Knapp, wife of the founder of the Metropolitan Life Insurance Company of New York. Mrs. Knapp was an amateur musician, and on one of her visits to the blind poetess she brought a melody she had composed.

"What does the tune say?" she asked Fanny Crosby, after playing it a few times. The blind woman responded immediately:

> Blessed assurance, Jesus is mine!
> Oh, what a foretaste of glory divine!
> Heir of salvation, purchase of God,
> Born of His Spirit, washed in His blood.

This method of composing words to an existing tune became a habit, and Miss Crosby used it in writing many of her seven thousand songs.

During the ministry of the Crusades and *The Hour of Decision* broadcasts, several hymns have been used as "theme songs." "Blessed Assurance" is one that seems to have lasted longer than the others. It has always been a favorite of mine. It is an ideal song of testimony which tells the unending peace and joy of the person who knows that God has accepted him because of what Jesus Christ has done on his behalf.

As well as I can remember, we began to use this song with Crusade choirs as early as 1948 in such places as Ocean City, New Jersey, and Baltimore, Maryland. My first wife, Billie, was playing the organ then—our family had not yet arrived—and together we worked out the changes of tempo and the high ending which became a trademark of Crusade music.

Admittedly, "Blessed Assurance" does not seem to have a clear outline or progression of thought. It is not a strong doctrinal presentation. Rather, it is a succession of completely personal, almost rambling expressions by an individual who *knows* that he or she has found life in Christ. In happiness and freedom one sings, "Blessed assurance, Jesus is mine!" The singer is convinced of having experienced a sample of heaven—a "foretaste of glory."

Both the second and third stanzas begin with the reminder that when we truly accept Jesus as Lord, we submit our wills to Him. At first this may seem to mean that we have lost our personal freedom. But we soon discover that this yielded life brings peace and rest, "delight and rapture."

Some criticize our simple Gospel songs by claiming that they are too selfish and personal in content. But becoming a Christian is a completely personal thing. I was converted when, as a teenager, it dawned on me that John 3:16 could be read this way: "For God so loved Cliff, that He gave His only begotten Son, that if Cliff would believe on Him, he would have everlasting life."

This is why I love to sing, "This is *my* story, this is *my* song, praising my Savior all the day long."

There is one short quotation on the side of Fanny Crosby's gravestone that is easily missed by the casual observer. It is a phrase that was spoken by Christ at Bethany after Mary the sister of Lazarus had anointed Him with a very costly perfume. When some objected to the "wasting" of the ointment, Jesus replied: "*She has done what she could*" (Mark 14:8).

I'm convinced that our Lord accepted the offering of Fanny Crosby in the same way. Her hymns contain the sweet aroma of her love for Christ. If she had written only this one song, it would have been enough to merit the approval of her Lord.

Prayer for the Day:

Dear Savior, I am grateful that You gave Fanny Crosby, and so many other hymn writers, the ability to craft songs that help proclaim Your great mercies. In the same way, make my praises and prayers an offering to You.

And Can It Be?

Charles Wesley, 1739

Thomas Campbell, 1825

1. And can it be that I should gain an in - terest
2. He left His Fa - ther's throne a - bove, so free, so
3. Long my im - pris - oned spir - it lay, fast bound in
4. No con - dem - na - tion now I dread; Je sus, and

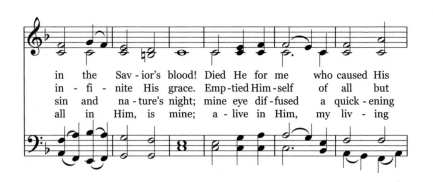

in the Sav - ior's blood! Died He for me who caused His
in - fi - nite His grace. Emp - tied Him - self of all but
sin and na - ture's night; mine eye dif - fused a quick - ening
all in Him, is mine; a - live in Him, my liv - ing

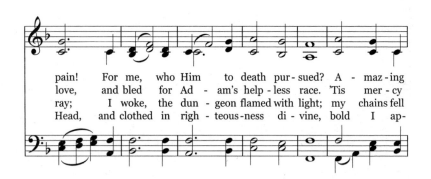

pain! For me, who Him to death pur - sued? A - maz - ing
love, and bled for Ad - am's help - less race. 'Tis mer - cy
ray; I woke, the dun - geon flamed with light; my chains fell
Head, and clothed in righ - teous - ness di - vine, bold I ap-

love! How can it be that Thou, my God, shouldst
all, im - mense and free, for O my God, it
off, my heart was free, I rose, went forth, and
proach the e - ter - nal throne, and claim the crown, through

die for me? A - maz - ing love! How can it
found out me! 'Tis mer - cy all, im-mense and
fol - lowed Thee. My chains fell off, my heart was
Christ, my own. Bold I ap - proach th'e - ter - nal

A - maz - ing love! How
'Tis mer - cy all, im -
My chains fell off, my
Bold I ap-proach th'e -

be that Thou, my God, shouldst die for me?
free, for O my God, it found out me!
free, I rose, went forth, and fol - lowed Thee.
throne, and claim the crown, through Christ, my own.

can it be that Thou, my God,
mense and free, for O my God,
heart was free, I rose, went forth,
ter - nal throne, and claim the crown,

And Can It Be?

Hymn story by Cliff Barrows

One of the most gripping songs about salvation is "And Can It Be?" The poem presents the drama of our redemption in two parts: first, the Lord's sacrifice to provide our salvation; and second, our experience when we accept His offering for us.

Not many hymns begin with a question as does this one. However, it is not an expression of doubt but of wonder and awe. How can it be that the shedding of Jesus' blood two thousand years ago is relevant to me today? How was it possible for the Son of God to have died for me? Why should our Lord empty Himself of all His divine glory and become a man, in order to save "Adam's helpless race"? Another stanza says that even the angels—including Gabriel, who is called the "first-born seraph"—try in vain to understand.

Charles Wesley, author of this hymn, may have been thinking of the earlier words of Isaac Watts:

> Alas, and did my Savior bleed?
> And did my Sovereign die?
> Would He devote that sacred head
> For such a worm as I?

Watts's attempt to explain the mystery is also limited to an expression of wonder: "Amazing pity! grace unknown! and love beyond degree!"

It is Wesley's advice that we do not waste time in a fruitless attempt to understand in full. It is beyond the comprehension of angels. Let us simply accept the fact of God's love and then lift our hearts in adoration to Christ.

This is the mystery of Christ's death. What does it mean in the experience of the individual believer?

There is considerable evidence that this hymn was written by Charles Wesley soon after his own conversion. Looking back, he sees himself as a prisoner in a dark dungeon, chained by the *sins* which he had committed and even more made captive by the sin which was a part of his very nature. The Gospel of Christ—the Good News that Christ had died to meet his need—seemed to flood the dungeon with light, break the chains, and set him free. His feeling of guilt was gone. For the first time he seemed to be really alive, because he possessed the supernatural life of Jesus Christ! He could face the final judgment unafraid because he was clothed in the very righteousness of Christ.

It may sound as if this were the dramatic experience of one who was rescued from a life of terrible sin and degradation. But, at the time of his conversion, Charles Wesley had already been a rector in the Church of England for three years; he had just returned from a term as missionary to Georgia in the New World. Even before that, he and his brother John had earned the derisive name "Methodist" because of the disciplined life which they imposed on themselves and other members of the "Holy Club" at Oxford University. But, in all this religious activity, he had never found spiritual peace; he was not convinced that the life of Christ was really his!

When our evangelistic Crusades were held in London, we often drove past the location on Aldersgate Street where history says that the Wesleys found Christian assurance for themselves. Nearby is the Wesley home and the chapel they built for worship.

Charles Wesley's crisis experience occurred on May 20, 1738. He had been sick in body as well as in spirit. It seemed that God spoke to him through a vision. According to his journal, this confrontation took place after reading the Bible for some time. Following is his account:

> At midnight I gave myself up to Christ: assured I was safe, sleeping or waking. Had continued experience of his power to overcome all temptations; and confessed, with joy and surprise, that he was able to do exceedingly abundantly for me, above what I can ask or think.

Two thousand years ago, when Jesus said to Nicodemus, "You must be born again," He was talking to one of the leaders of the Jewish community, one of the most respected men of that day. I recently heard of a seventy-one-year-old minister who, after spending fifty years in the service of the church, had just come to know Jesus Christ as his Savior.

Like the experience Charles Wesley describes in this hymn, the old minister learned personally to know God. He realized, as we must also, that "doing good" means nothing to God. To accept Christ's love and sacrifice for himself was to find the source of the Christian life.

Prayer for the Day:

Heavenly Father, thank You for sending Your Son Jesus to die on the cross for my sins. I need Your forgiveness each day, and I trust in You to guide me as I seek to live for You.

Holy Spirit, Breathe on Me

Edwin Hatch, 1878;
adapted B.B. McKinney, 1937

B.B. McKinney, 1937

1. Ho - ly Spir - it, breathe on me, un - til my heart is clean;
2. Ho - ly Spir - it, breathe on me, my stub - born will sub - due;
3. Ho - ly Spir - it, breathe on me, fill me with power di - vine;
4. Ho - ly Spir - it, breathe on me, till I am all Thine own;

let sun - shine fill its in - most part, with not a cloud be - tween.
teach me in words of li - ving flame what Christ would have me do.
kin - dle a flame of love and zeal with - in this heart of mine.
un - til my will is lost in Thine, to live for Thee a - lone.

Breathe on me, breathe on me, Ho - ly Spir - it, breathe on me;

take Thou my heart, cleanse eve - ry part, Ho - ly Spir - it, breathe on me.

Holy Spirit, Breathe on Me
Hymn story by Cliff Barrows

Both because of his size and accomplishment, B.B. McKinney stood out as a giant in the field of Gospel music during the early twentieth century. McKinney was a big man—more than six feet tall and two hundred pounds in weight—with a large, warm-hearted personality to match. He was both a winsome and commanding figure, whether he was singing a solo, directing an evangelistic choir, or managing an office.

His contributions to the Southern Baptist ministry accorded him a title as "the father of church music among Southern Baptists." After teaching at Southwestern Seminary and serving as assistant pastor of the Travis Avenue Baptist Church in Fort Worth, Texas, he became secretary of the newly organized Church Music Department at Baptist headquarters in Nashville, Tennessee. Here he edited the first hymnals to be widely used by Southern Baptists, and initiated the ministry in church music.

Besides this educational ministry, he exercised a personal talent for composing. Among the 150 songs for which Dr. McKinney wrote both words and music, there are at least two which are adaptations of earlier hymns by other writers. One of these, "Holy Spirit, Breathe on Me," gives us McKinney's personal understanding of the hymn "Breathe on Me, Breath of God." The original was written in 1878 by Edwin Hatch, a professor at Oxford University.

Borrowing from earlier sources, as McKinney did in this instance, is a fairly common practice. Many of Isaac Watts's hymns are adaptations of the Jewish hymns we call psalms; for instance, "O God, Our Help in Ages Past" is based on Psalm 90. Similarly, "Just As I Am, Thine Own to Be" is a youth version of "Just As I Am, Without One Plea." J. Wilbur Chapman's "Our Great Savior" quotes many phrases from Charles Wesley's "Jesus, Lover of My Soul." I believe it should be regarded as a compliment to the earlier hymn when a subsequent writer wants to restate its truth in his own words.

At first glance, both these titles, "Holy Spirit, Breathe on Me" and "Breathe on Me, Breath of God," may seem a bit odd. To personify and address deity so directly may appear presumptuous. However, in the original language of the New Testament, the word for spirit is *pneuma*, which means "wind" or "breath." On the day of Pentecost, the Holy Spirit's coming was accompanied with "*a sound from heaven,* as of a rushing mighty wind" (Acts 2:2). In anticipation of that day, John 20:22 says that Jesus "breathed" on His disciples and said, "Receive the Holy Spirit."

The verses of this hymn tell what the Holy Spirit does for the Christian, because He dwells in the believer's heart. The words "Breathe on me, until my heart is clean" in stanza one, remind us that it is God's Spirit who daily cleanses or sanctifies us, causing us to be more and more like Jesus Christ. Paul said to the Corinthians: "But you were washed, but you were sanctified, but you were justified in the name of the Lord Jesus and by the Spirit of our God" (1 Corinthians 6:11).

It is the Holy Spirit who also leads us to consecrate ourselves to Christ. "Holy Spirit, breathe on me, my stubborn will subdue," the stanzas continue. In the Scriptures, Ephesians 5:18 reiterates this in another way, "Do not get drunk on wine, which leads to debauchery. Instead, be filled with the Spirit" (NIV). An individual who is under the influence of stimulants does not have control over his or her own actions but is dominated by the effects of the alcohol or drugs. When we are filled with the Holy Spirit, we are under His complete control to do the perfect will of God.

The third stanza states that it is the Holy Spirit who gives us spiritual power to become mature personalities capable of serving God more effectively. So we sing in a spirit of prayer, "Holy Spirit, breathe on me, fill me with power divine." Christ promised His disciples, "You will receive power when the Holy Spirit comes on you; and you will be my witnesses" (Acts 1:8, NIV). It was this power that enabled the early Christians to spread the Gospel throughout the known world within their lifetimes. The same resource for effective ministry is available today.

As we live each day, the Holy Spirit wants to do these same things for us, and in the same order. First, He would cleanse us from sin; second, He wants to help us dedicate ourselves completely to God; and finally, He desires to give us all the resources of God so that we may live triumphantly.

Prayer for the Day:

God, You promise Your Spirit to me as Your follower. Help me to rely not on my own strength or intellect but on Your power as You infuse me each day. Cleanse my heart of sin and help me to live triumphantly for You.

Let the Lower Lights Be Burning

Philip Paul Bliss, 1871

Philip Paul Bliss, 1871

1. Bright-ly beams our Fa-ther's mer-cy from His light-house ev - er - more,
2. Dark the night of sin has set-tled, loud the an - gry bil-lows roar;
3. Trim your fee - ble lamp, my broth-er! Some poor sail - or, tem-pest tossed,

but to us He gives the keep-ing of the lights a - long the shore.
ea - ger eyes are watch-ing, long-ing, for the lights a - long the shore.
try-ing now to make the har-bor, in the dark-ness may be lost.

Refrain

Let the low - er lights be burn-ing! Send a gleam a-cross the wave!

Some poor faint - ing, strug-gling sea-man you may res-cue, you may save.

Let the Lower Lights Be Burning
Hymn story by Billy Graham

D.L. Moody, the great evangelist of the nineteenth century, often told this story to illustrate each Christian's responsibility to point others to our Lord.

> On a dark, stormy night when the waves rolled like mountains and not a star could be seen, a large passenger boat cautiously edged toward the Cleveland harbor. The pilot knew that, in the inky darkness, he could only find the harbor channel by keeping two lower shore lights in line with the main beacon.
>
> "Are you sure this is Cleveland?" asked the captain, seeing only one light from the lighthouse.
>
> "Quite sure, sir," replied the pilot.
>
> "Where are the lower lights?" he asked.
>
> "Gone out, sir," was the reply.
>
> "Can you make the harbor?"
>
> "We must or perish, sir!"
>
> With a strong hand and a brave heart, the old pilot turned the wheel. But alas! In the darkness he missed the channel, the boat crashed on the rocks and many lives were lost.

D.L. Moody's closing words were: "Brethren, the Master will take care of the great lighthouse; *let us keep the lower lights burning.*" Later, the story became a poem set to music, both written by Philip P. Bliss, the song evangelist who worked with Moody and also with Moody's friend, Major D.W. Whittle. This was the favorite hymn of the early-twentieth-century evangelist Billy Sunday.

Many people seem to believe that their life and their witness do not count for much in God's kingdom. But every one of us contacts certain people every day—our neighbors, a friend in the shop or the office, the paper boy or the garbage collector—and for those particular persons, we may provide the only opportunity to hear a personal witness of the Gospel. Unless we tell them, they will not hear!

During a large rally in the Los Angeles, California, Coliseum, at a prearranged signal a switch was pulled and the entire stadium was plunged into darkness. Then the speaker struck a small match and encouraged each of the 100,000 people present to do the same. In a moment the light from those tiny, flickering matches illuminated the entire amphitheater. Our light of Christian witness may be small, but it does count, especially when it is added to that of other believers.

In explaining the imagery found in this Gospel song, we might say that the great beam of the lighthouse represents the Bible, a Christian magazine, a Gospel broadcast, or some outstanding preacher in a historic church pulpit. But each of us is a "lower light" whose gleam is needed to point lost souls to the safety of the harbor, Jesus Christ.

The last stanza of this hymn may not be immediately understood by today's younger generation. It refers to the kerosene lamps and lanterns which were common in Bliss's day and which were still being used in our house and barn when I was a boy on the farm. I remember that it was important that the wick be trimmed regularly—that all the charred part be removed—so that the lamp would burn brightly and evenly and not smoke up the protecting glass.

Each of us has only one light to give to the world. So it is important that we keep it burning brightly, and that all the charrings of sin and selfishness be taken away. This is the same spiritual experience that Jesus talked about in John 15:2: *"He cuts off every branch in me that bears no fruit, while every branch that does bear fruit he prunes so that it will be even more fruitful"* (NIV). Trimming the wick—like pruning a vine—may be painful, especially to our pride, but it results in a brighter witness and a more fruitful life.

The light of the life of Philip Bliss—author of this hymn—burned brightly, but only for a few years. At the age of thirty-eight, while traveling to Chicago for an engagement at the Moody Tabernacle, both he and his wife were killed in a train accident. Yet, through the many hymns he wrote, his lamp of Christian influence still shines and lights the way to faith in God. *"Let your light shine before others, that they may see your good deeds and glorify your Father in heaven"* (Matthew 5:16, NIV).

Prayer for the Day:

Dear Jesus, trim away the things in my life that may dim my light and prevent others from finding the safe harbor You offer. Help me to add my own small flame to that of other believers to create a spiritual fire that lights the world and glorifies You.

To God Be the Glory

Fanny Jane Crosby, 1875   William Howard Doane, 1875

1. To God be the glo - ry, great things He hath done; so
2. O per - fect re-demp-tion, the pur-chase of blood, to
3. Great things He hath taught us, great things He hath done, and

loved He the world that He gave us His Son, who yield - ed His life an a -
ev - ery be-liev - er the prom-ise of God; the vil - est of-fend-er who
great our re-joic -ing through Je - sus the Son; but pur - er, and high-er, and

tone-ment for sin, and o -pened the life-gate that all may go in.
tru - ly be-lieves, that mo-ment from Je - sus a par-don re - ceives.
great - er will be our won-der, our vic-tory, when Je - sus we see.

Refrain

Praise the Lord, praise the Lord, let the earth hear His voice! Praise the Lord,

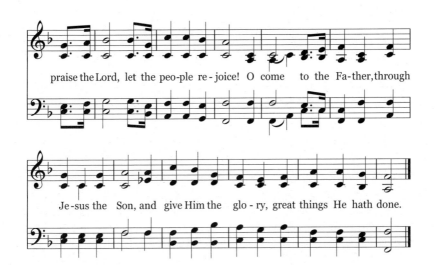

praise the Lord, let the peo-ple re - joice! O come to the Fa-ther, through

Je-sus the Son, and give Him the glo - ry, great things He hath done.

To God Be the Glory
Hymn story by Cliff Barrows

If a hymn dies, can it live again? The life-story of "To God Be the Glory" proves that the answer is "yes!" Originally composed in America sometime before 1875, it was almost immediately forgotten in its native land. In 1954, however, "To God Be the Glory" was rediscovered and acclaimed as a new favorite.

In Great Britain this same hymn never faded into oblivion as it did in the United States. I had heard it sung there in 1952 during one of our early visits. Later, it was suggested for inclusion in the songbook we were compiling for the London Crusade of 1954. Because of its strong text of praise and its attractive melody, I agreed. We introduced the hymn during the early days of those meetings in Harringay Arena. As a result, Billy Graham asked that we repeat it often because he was impressed with the enthusiastic participation of the audience. In the closing weeks of the Crusade it became our theme hymn, repeated almost every night. The words well expressed our praise to God, who was doing wondrous things in Britain.

Returning to America, we brought the hymn with us and used it first in the Nashville, Tennessee, Crusade of August 1954. It was quickly adopted by many church groups and was included in several hymnals, including the *Baptist Hymnal* (Southern Baptist) and *Trinity Hymnal* (Orthodox Presbyterian).

Why "To God Be the Glory" was so late in achieving recognition in its homeland may always remain a mystery. It is not mentioned in the writings of either Fanny Crosby, author of the words, or W.H. Doane, composer of the music. Evidently the song leader Ira D. Sankey took it to Great Britain when he went there with evangelist D.L. Moody in 1873. Sankey included it in his *Sacred Songs and Solos*, a hymnbook first published in England in 1874.

For some unknown reason, the song did not appear in the important *Gospel Hymns* series of books which Sankey published in America after his return from Britain in 1875. Through the years, "To God Be the Glory" *has* been included in several American hymnals. But until 1954, it failed to find its rightful place in the singing of our congregations.

Of all the songs that have been popularized through Crusade activity, we are most happy about this one. Its testimony should rebound in the heart of every Christian; every area of a person's life should reflect this witness, "To God Be the Glory."

Everyone—Christian or non-Christian—tries to find meaning in life. Modern existentialists, atheists, and agnostics (and even a few who call themselves Christians) are trying to find this meaning *within himself or herself.* But the true answer to this quest is defined in the *Westminster Catechism*: "The chief end of man is to glorify God, and to enjoy Him forever." In other words, the reason for humanity's creation and the whole purpose of living is to express praise of God, with our lips and with our life.

We give God glory because of His love, a love which provided redemption for all people. The Apostle Paul exclaimed, "*God forbid that I should boast except in the cross of our Lord Jesus Christ*" (Galatians 6:14). We bring nothing to our own salvation; it is all of God. Therefore, we can take no credit for it. To God be the glory!

In another passage, Paul reminds us: "*For you were bought at a price; therefore glorify God in your body and in your spirit, which are God's*" (1 Corinthians 6:20). This is the biblical answer to the seeking existentialist. Each day's experiences have ultimate meaning only if we acknowledge that we are God's, and that each act and each thought should glorify Him. To God be the glory!

Billy Graham has often reminded us team members that this is especially true in the full-time Christian vocations. God has chosen to use *people* to spread His Good News, the Gospel. Because we live in a Madison Avenue world of culture and communication, the names of preachers and evangelists are sometimes advertised widely. But we will be in serious trouble if we imagine that the Crusade ministry is possible because of us or our talents. It is all of God, who has declared, "*My glory I will not give to another*" (Isaiah 42:8). To God be the glory!

A challenge for each day of each Christian's life is found in Matthew 5:16: "*Let your good deeds shine out for all to see, so that everyone will praise your heavenly Father*" (NLT). We should be thankful if others feel that we have been gracious and loving in our relations with them. But we dare not keep the praise for ourselves! It is God who enables us to be Christlike. To God be the glory!

Prayer for the Day:

Heavenly Father, I praise You for Your mercies, which Jesus demonstrated by going to the cross for my sins. Thank You for working in and through my life, that others may see You. I pray that everything I do today would give glory and honor to You and You alone.

Wherever He Leads, I'll Go

B.B. McKinney, 1936

B.B. McKinney, 1936

1. "Take up thy cross and fol-low Me," I heard my Mas-ter say;
2. He drew me clo-ser to His side, I sought His will to know,
3. It may be through the sha-dows dim, or o'er the stor-my sea,
4. My heart, my life, my all I bring to Christ who loves me so;

"I gave My life to ran-som thee, sur-ren-der your all to-day."
and in that will I now a-bide, wher-e-ver He leads I'll go.
I take my cross and fol-low Him, wher-e-ver He lea-deth me.
he is my Mas-ter, Lord, and King, wher-e-ver He leads I'll go.

Refrain

Wher-e-ver He leads I'll go, wher-e-ver He leads I'll go,

I'll fol-low my Christ who loves me so, wher-e-ver He leads I'll go.

Wherever He Leads, I'll Go
Hymn story by Billy Graham

In January of 1936, the Southern Baptist songwriter B.B. McKinney was leading the music at the Alabama Sunday School Convention, which was held that year in the town of Clanton. The featured speaker was the Reverend R.S. Jones, McKinney's friend of many years, who because of ill health had recently returned from missionary service in Brazil.

The two men were visiting over dinner one evening when Mr. Jones revealed to Dr. McKinney that his physicians would not allow him to return to South America. When asked about his future plans, the missionary said, "I don't know, but wherever He leads I'll go." The words stuck in Dr. McKinney's mind, and before the convention's evening session began, he had written both the words and music of this song. At the close of Mr. Jones' message, Dr. McKinney related this story and sang "Wherever He Leads, I'll Go" to the congregation.

The opening words of the song, "Take up thy cross and follow Me," contain one of Jesus' most penetrating challenges to His disciples—a statement so significant that it is found in each of the four gospels. Luke 9:23 states: *"If anyone desires to come after Me, let him deny himself, and take up his cross daily, and follow Me."*

In the New Living Translation the same verse begins, *"If any of you wants to be my follower, you must turn from your selfish ways."* J.B. Phillips paraphrased it this way: *"If anyone wants to follow in my footsteps, he must give up all right to himself."*

The original Greek New Testament has an even stronger inference than any of these. There the words used for "deny himself" can be translated "I don't even know that person!" This kind of selflessness is hard for most people to understand. Even when Christians understand it, performance is hard to achieve! Just how does this attitude manifest itself in everyday life?

A member of your church may be asked to teach a Sunday school class. Because of inborn timidity, the natural response is to refuse and even to believe that the refusal is a sign of humility. But, in the same situation, the dedicated Christian will accept the opportunity to serve, saying, "Who is that shy and fearful self? I don't know any such person!" This is "denying one's self," and it is a healthy attitude, psychologically and spiritually!

And what does it mean to "take up your cross"? Does this phrase suggest that the Christian should expect to carry heavy burdens? I believe it implies much more than that. The cross was an instrument of public execution. If Christ were speaking today, He would say, "Take up your electric chair and follow me." The Apostle Paul explained this command when he said, "*My old self has been crucified with Christ. It is no longer I who live, but Christ lives in me*" (Galatians 2:20, NLT). It is our inner self-centeredness which dies when we yield to a higher will than our own. God's will replaces ours, and then Christ truly lives within us.

Living on this higher plane provides a new response to the situations of life. When a cruel and false accusation is made against us, our natural reaction is to fight back, to vindicate ourselves. If the story wasn't true, we feel justified in returning the insult. But to the person living on a Christ-centered level, the "self" who was criticized is dead—crucified. How can a dead "self" talk back?

The reality of the indwelling Christ is demonstrated by selflessness in all the important decisions of life. Such a dedication is what the hymn "Wherever He Leads, I'll Go" is mostly all about. Of course, we may have a personal interest in one vocation or another or a preference to live in this location or that. But when we "follow Christ," we must ask ourselves, "What decision does He want me to make? Where does Christ want me to serve? And how?"

For some, it will be a glorious privilege to serve God as a pastor, missionary, an evangelist, a teacher, or a church musician. This hymn is certainly a good one to sing when a challenge for missionary service is given. But don't forget that its inspiration came from a missionary who could not return to the field! The Rev. Jones spent the rest of his life serving with the Southern Baptist Relief and Annuity Board.

Other Christians too will have the no-less-glorious honor of serving Christ as a doctor, a teacher, an office worker, or a farmer. In every instance, our life's work should be determined by God's call, not just our whims and desires. When this is true, even washing dishes becomes a sacrament, as proclaimed in the motto my wife has posted in her kitchen: "Divine services conducted here three times daily."

Prayer for the Day:

Jesus, show me Your will for my life. Remind me daily that Your calling is not always to public ministry but sometimes to a private mission. Let me always be willing to forget myself and follow You.

Trust and Obey

John Henry Sammis, ca. 1887

Daniel Brink Towner, ca. 1887

1. When we walk with the Lord in the light of His Word, what a glo - ry He
2. Not   a shad-ow can rise, not a cloud in the skies, but His smile quick-ly
3. Not   a bur-den we bear, not a sor-row we share, but our toil He doth
4. But   we nev-er can prove the de-lights of His love un-til   all on the
5. Then in   fel-low-ship sweet we will sit at His   feet, or we'll walk by His

sheds on our way! While we do His good will,   He   a-bides with us still,
drives it a - way; not   a doubt nor a   fear,   not   a sigh nor a   tear,
rich - ly re - pay; not   a grief nor a   loss,   not   a frown nor a cross,
al - tar we lay; for the fa - vor He shows, for the joy He be-stows,
side   in the way; what He says we will   do,   where He sends we will   go;

Refrain

and with all   who will trust and o - bey.
can   a - bide while we trust and o - bey.
but   is blessed if   we trust and o - bey.   Trust and o - bey, for there's
are   for them who will trust and o - bey.
nev - er fear, on - ly   trust and o - bey.

no oth-er   way to be hap-py in   Je-sus, but to   trust and o - bey.

Trust and Obey
Hymn story by Cliff Barrows

I first learned to know the great songs of the church as a boy in Sunday school in Ceres, California. Sometime later I was drafted to be the third member of a family trio, singing with my two younger sisters. It seemed to me then that we were too often called upon to perform at church services, youth rallies and camps, and even at weddings and funerals!

Consequently, as a growing boy, I must admit that hymn-singing was occasionally more pain than pleasure. But in later life, the hymnbook became one of my most important resources for personal worship. Today, I am thankful that I was required to memorize so many hymns at an early age. They will probably never leave my subconscious.

One of my longtime favorites, which we always included in Crusade songbooks, is "Trust and Obey." The music for this song was composed by D.B. Towner, the first director of music at Moody Bible Institute in Chicago. The inspiration for the hymn's writing came in 1886 during an occasion when Towner was leading singing for D.L. Moody in Brockton, Massachusetts. In a testimony service which took place, he heard a young man say, "I am not quite sure but I am going to trust, and I am going to obey."

Towner jotted down the words and sent them to his friend J.H. Sammis, a Presbyterian minister, who developed the idea into a full hymn. The refrain came first—it is a capsule version of the entire song—and the verses later.

The song emphasizes the two aspects of being a Christian—faith and good works. And it places them in proper order! We come to Christ without any plea but that He shed His blood for us. "*God saved you by his grace when you believed. And you can't take credit for this; it is a gift from God*" (Ephesians 2:8, NLT).

But after we trust in Christ, our faith must be translated into action. Because God loves us and we love Him, we seek to obey Him and to do His will in every realm of our lives. As James asks, "*What good is it to say you have faith, when you don't do anything to show that you really do have faith?*" (James 2:14, CEV).

I am afraid that some Christians are tempted to think negatively about a commitment of obedience to God. To submit to the commands "to die to self" and "to present your body a living sacrifice" sounds like such a painful thing.

But the truth is clearly stated in this hymn. "We never can prove [experience] the delights of His love, until all on the altar we lay. There's no other way to be happy ... but to trust and obey." Do we imagine that God who loves us so much would wish us anything less than that which brings us complete fulfillment in life? We can trust God to manage our affairs better than we can ourselves.

D.L. Moody said on one occasion: "The blood [of Christ] alone makes us safe. The Word [to God] alone makes us sure. Obedience [to God] makes us happy." What a formula for a poised and successful life! The death and resurrection of Christ provides a full and free salvation. God's Word assures us that it is settled for all eternity. And allowing God to order our lives each day ensures complete serenity and happiness.

Somehow I always associate the message of "Trust and Obey" with Dawson Trotman of The Navigators, who worked with us for several years before his untimely death.

"Daws" often brought a message on the TNT of Christian service—"Trust 'n' Tackle." The "trust" in this motto implies a complete, childlike confidence in our heavenly Father and an obedience to Him in all of life's activities. Then we can be assured of God's strength bolstering us to tackle any challenge that may appear. God will see us through!

Prayer for the Day:

Thank You, Lord, for providing Your Word to show us how to live in complete obedience. Help me to trust You in all things and to follow You daily. I know that You will provide the strength I need for every challenge.

Ivory Palaces

Henry Barraclough

Henry Barraclough,
arr. Donald P. Hustad

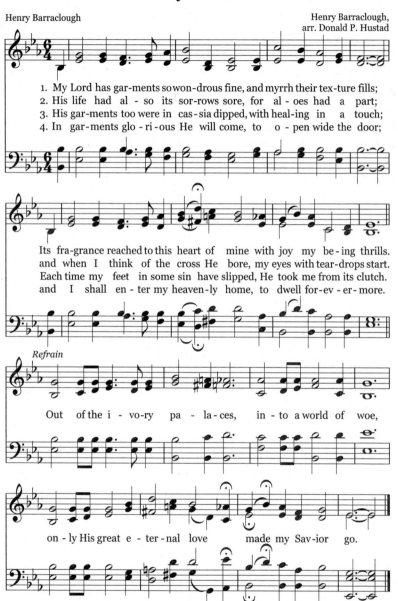

1. My Lord has gar-ments so won-drous fine, and myrrh their tex-ture fills;
2. His life had al - so its sor-rows sore, for al - oes had a part;
3. His gar-ments too were in cas-sia dipped, with heal-ing in a touch;
4. In gar-ments glo - ri-ous He will come, to o - pen wide the door;

Its fra-grance reached to this heart of mine with joy my be - ing thrills.
and when I think of the cross He bore, my eyes with tear-drops start.
Each time my feet in some sin have slipped, He took me from its clutch.
and I shall en - ter my heaven-ly home, to dwell for-ev - er-more.

Refrain

Out of the i - vo-ry pa - la-ces, in - to a world of woe,

on - ly His great e - ter - nal love made my Sav-ior go.

Ivory Palaces
Hymn story by Billy Graham

The Gospel song "Ivory Palaces" was written very near to my home in the mountains of North Carolina. In the summer of 1915, the famous evangelist Dr. J. Wilbur Chapman was preaching at the Presbyterian conference grounds at Montreat. With him were the song leader Charles M. Alexander, soloist Albert Brown, and their pianist Henry Barraclough. Barraclough, the author of this hymn, was a twenty-four-year-old Britisher; he had met Chapman the previous year during a preaching mission in England.

During the conference, the evangelist spoke one evening on the forty-fifth Psalm. He believed, as I do, that this is a prophetic, "Messianic" psalm which speaks of the relationship of Christ, the bridegroom, to His bride, the church.

The eighth verse of the psalm was Dr. Chapman's text: *"All Your garments are scented with myrrh and aloes and cassia, out of the ivory palaces, by which they have made You glad."*

The oriental spices and perfumes mentioned here were used for many purposes. They were often poured on clothing so that their delightful odor seemed to be part of the very texture of the cloth. Following the suggestions of these provocative phrases, Dr. Chapman developed his sermon on the symbolism of the perfumed garments of an oriental bridegroom.

Myrrh was an exotic perfume associated with ecstasy and joy; it represents the beauty of the person of Christ—that beauty which attracts us to Him. Aloe was a bitter herb used in embalming, which should remind us that our Lord had many sorrows during His lifetime, culminating in a shameful and painful death on the cross. Cassia was a spicy perfume that was also a medication; Jesus Christ is like a potion that heals us from the wounds of sin when we look to Him in repentance.

After the evening service, "Charlie" Alexander and Henry Barraclough drove some friends to the Blue Ridge YMCA hostel a few miles away. Sitting in the front seat of the car, young Barraclough thought about the message, and the four short phrases of the refrain began to take shape in his mind. When they stopped at a little village store, he quickly wrote them down on a "visiting card"—the only paper available. Returning to the conference hotel, he worked out the first three stanzas, using the outline of Chapman's message. The following morning Mrs. Alexander and Mr. Brown sang the new hymn in the Montreat conference session.

Later, Dr. Chapman suggested that Barraclough add a fourth verse, reminding us that one day Christ will come again wearing the same glorious garments. I believe that through all eternity we will be reminded of the beauty of our Lord, of His suffering for us, and of the forgiveness and cleansing which He has made possible.

Henry Barraclough was not a prolific song writer. "Ivory Palaces" was his only masterpiece, but it has been sung around the world. After Dr. Chapman's death, Barraclough adopted the evangelist's country, America, as his own. He also became associated with Chapman's denomination and served the Presbyterian Church (U.S.A.) for more than fifty years.

It was Albert Brown—one member of the duet that first sang "Ivory Palaces"—who first introduced Cliff Barrows to me in 1945. I was speaking at a youth night service at the Ben Lippen Conference Grounds in North Carolina. When the regular song leader could not appear, Mr. Brown suggested that we use two young musicians named Cliff and Billie Barrows who were visiting there on their honeymoon. That was the beginning of our many years of fellowship in God's service.

In our Crusades, Bev Shea often sang this hymn, sometimes accompanied by Cliff Barrows and the choir. We do not suppose that heaven actually consists of "ivory palaces"; this is merely the oriental imagery which is used to try to describe the beauty of our Lord's home, from which He departed to live among people on earth. Every time I hear this refrain, I am humbled by the truth that Jesus—the object of all the worship in heaven—willingly assumed all the limitations and suffering of a man. Why? Because He loved us so much.

> Out of the ivory palaces,
> Into a world of woe,
> Only His great, eternal love.
> Made my Savior go.

Prayer for the Day:

Dear Jesus, I am grateful and humbled that You left Your heavenly kingdom to come to earth as a man. May I never forget the sorrow and suffering that You took on Yourself for my sake, simply because of Your love.

Revive Us Again

William Paton Mackay, 1863

John Jenkins Husband, ca. 1815

1. We praise Thee, O God, for the Son of Thy love,
2. We praise Thee, O God, for Thy Spir - it of light,
3. All glo - ry and praise to the Lamb that was slain,
4. Re - vive us a - gain: fill each heart with Thy love;

for Je - sus who died and is now gone a - bove.
Who has shown us our Sav - ior and scat - tered our night.
Who has borne all our sins and has cleansed ev - ery stain.
may each soul be re - kin - dled with fire from a - bove.

Refrain

Hal - le - lu - jah, Thine the glo - ry! Hal - le - lu - jah, A - men!

Hal - le - lu - jah, Thine the glo - ry! Re - vive us a - gain.

Revive Us Again
Hymn story by Cliff Barrows

"Revive Us Again" is a Gospel song that we used in almost every evangelistic Crusade for decades. When we sang it, we often reverted to the ancient practice of antiphony, which was common in the performance of the Hebrew psalms. In the refrain, the audience on one side of the auditorium or stadium would sing "Hallelujah!" and those on the other side would echo "Thine the glory," and so on until the final phrase "Revive us again," which we sang in unison.

There were technical problems, of course! Because of the size of the congregations and the relatively slow speed at which sound travels, it was sometimes difficult to stay together. Nevertheless, even without the help of organ and piano, it provided a thrilling experience of praise in song.

Sometimes we sang the hymn responsively over long distances. In our final meeting in Sydney, Australia, in 1959, the first phrase was sung by 80,000 people in the Royal Agriculture Society's Showground. They were answered by 70,000 people in the Cricket Ground, almost two blocks away. In 1955, by use of a telephone line relay, the folks in Bangor, North Wales, responded to the audience in Glasgow, Scotland.

A critic of hymns might point out that the text of this poem is a bit incongruous. It first appeared in 1875 under the Scripture verse, "*O Lord, revive thy work*" (Habakkuk 3:2, KJV). The reader's initial reaction is that it is a prayer for spiritual revival among God's people. Nevertheless, the first three stanzas consist entirely of praising God. Only the last stanza seems to conform to the thought of the title, and is a prayer that the church and each Christian in it might be renewed in faith and spiritual vigor. In the same way, the refrain echoes its paeans of praise over and over, and at the end—almost as an afterthought—there is the prayer "Revive us again."

We can be sure, however, that the author, William P. Mackay (a physician who became a Scottish Presbyterian minister), knew what he was doing. There is deep spiritual insight shown here, and we are reminded of the experience of the Israelites during the reign of Jehoshaphat (ca. 896 B.C.)

God's chosen people were being threatened by the Moabites and the Ammonites, and they were very much afraid. A word of encouragement was brought to King Jehoshaphat by Jahaziel, one of the musicians in the temple:

> *Thus says the Lord to you: "Do not be afraid nor dismayed because of this great multitude, for the battle is not yours, but*

God's. ... You will not need to fight in this battle. Position yourselves, stand still and see the salvation of the Lord, who is with you. (2 Chronicles 20:15, 17)

The story goes on:

> *And when he [Jehoshaphat] had consulted with the people, he appointed those who should sing to the Lord, and who should praise the beauty of holiness, as they went out before the army and were saying:*
>
>> *"Praise the Lord,*
>> *For His mercy endures forever."*
>
> *Now when they began to sing and to praise, the Lord set ambushes against the people of Ammon, Moab, and Mount Seir, who had come against Judah; and they were defeated.* (2 Chronicles 20:21–22)

The enemies of our souls are many, and we are often painfully aware of them—our own innate weaknesses, the world of allurements around us, and the devil, who appears sometimes as a "roaring lion" and sometimes as an "angel of light." Our potential for victory against these foes will not be found within ourselves; it is not even the result of our own holy desires. The source of our victory is found in God, and our resources are His own divine holiness and power. When we are properly conscious of God's attributes—as well as of our own weakness and vulnerability—and when we give Him glory, then His strength works through us. If you face a particularly heavy burden or a strong temptation today, lay it aside and sing a song of praise to God. "Revive Us Again" would be a good choice!

Prayer for the Day:

Help me, dear Father, to praise You today in spite of my trials and temptations. I know that victory in my life comes only through Your power. Keep me always mindful of Your love and grace as I give You the glory.

In My Heart There Rings a Melody

Elton M. Roth   Elton M. Roth

1. I have a song that Je-sus gave me, it was sent from heaven a-
2. I love the Christ who died on Cal-vary, for He washed my sins a-
3. 'Twill be my end-less theme in glo-ry, with the an-gels I will

bove; there nev-er was a sweet-er mel-o-dy, 'tis a
way; He put with-in my heart a mel-o-dy, and I
sing; 'twill be a song with glo-rious har-mo-ny, when the

Refrain

mel-o-dy of love.
know it's there to-day.   In my heart there rings a mel-o-dy, there
courts of heav-en ring.

rings a mel-o-dy with heav-en's har-mo-ny; in my heart there

rings a mel-o-dy, there rings a mel-o-dy of love.

In My Heart There Rings a Melody
Hymn story by Tedd Smith

Not many people are given a great singing voice, but everyone can have a song! The psalmist explains the source of the music in a Christian's life:

> I waited patiently for the Lord; and He inclined to me, and heard my cry. He also brought me up out of a horrible pit, out of the miry clay, and set my feet upon a rock, and established my steps. He has put a new song in my mouth—praise to our God; many will see it and fear, and will trust in the Lord. (Psalm 40:1–3)

This new song which God gives us may have no words whatever, no melody, no rhythm, and no harmony! This is a "song in the heart." The hymn title says, "In My Heart There Rings a Melody"; it is based on the words of the Apostle Paul in Ephesians 5:19: "*singing and making melody in your heart to the Lord.*"

What is the heart singing? The final phrase of the refrain describes it: It is a "melody of love"—God's love to us, and our love to God and to others. It is a song of joy—not merely happiness or pleasure, but an eternal joy that persists through all the sorrows and tragedies of life. It is also a song of peace and serenity that gives poise and maturity amid the pressures of our culture.

Someone has said, "If there were more singing Christians, there would be more Christians!" If this heart-song of love, joy, and peace is evident in our daily lives, we will become very conspicuous in our communities and in our daily life contacts. Others will want to know the secret of our victorious living. As the psalmist declared in the passage quoted previously, "*Many will see it and fear, and will trust in the Lord.*"

Elton Menno Roth, the hymn's writer, was for many years a distinguished church musician—singer, composer, and conductor. In the 1930s, after serious study with several prominent teachers, he organized professional choirs which achieved national recognition in their concert tours.

Roth once said that this hymn was written while he was conducting an evangelistic meeting in Texas. As he recalled:

> One hot summer afternoon I took a little walk to the cotton mill just outside of town. On my way back through the burning streets of this typical plantation village, I became weary with the oppressive heat, and paused at a church on the corner. The

door being open, I went in. There were no people in the pews, no minister in the pulpit. Everything was quiet, with a lingering sacred presence. I walked up and down the aisle and began singing, "In my heart there rings a melody," then hurried into the pastor's study to find some paper. I drew a staff and sketched the melody, remaining there for an hour or more to finish the song, both words and music.

That evening I introduced it by having over two hundred boys and girls sing it at the open air meeting, after which the audience joined in the singing. I was thrilled as it seemed my whole being was transformed into a song!

In my profession of church music, we hear a good deal of talk about the music which pleases God and which ministers to people. Like Roth, we must be concerned about the quality of our musical compositions, and our performance of them. But we dare not forget that God is more concerned about whether or not we have a song in our heart. It is this melody in a life which will convince other men and women that our Christian faith is vital and desirable.

Prayer for the Day:

You, Jesus, have given me a song in my heart because of Your salvation. Make this heart-song evident to those around me as I share Your love, joy, and peace with them. Use my life to show them how to trust You.

He the Pearly Gates Will Open

WORDS: Fredrick Arvid Blom, 1917
tr. Nathaniel Carlson, ca. 1935

Elsie Rebekah Ahlwen, 1930

1. Love di-vine, so great and won-drous, deep and might y, pure, sub-lime;
2. Like a dove when hunt-ed, fright-ened, as a wound-ed fawn was I,
3. Love di-vine, so great and won-drous: All my sins He then for gave,
4. In life's e-ven-tide, at twi-light, at His door I'll knock and wait;

com-ing from the heart of Je - sus: Just the same through test of time.
bro-ken heart-ed, yet He healed me: He will heed the sin-ner's cry.
I will sing His praise for-ev - er, for His blood, His power to save.
by the pre cious love of Je - sus, I shall en - ter heav en's gate.

Refrain

He the pearl-y gates will o - pen, so that I may en-ter in;

for He pur-chased my re - demp -tion, and for-gave me all my sin.

He the Pearly Gates Will Open
Hymn story by Cliff Barrows

In preparation for a series of Crusade services in Scandinavia in 1955, we were looking for something in Swedish to sing. Someone suggested "Han skall öppna pärleporten," or translated, "He the Pearly Gates Will Open." Because the song is a natural duet, Bev Shea graciously asked me to sing it with him. It is one of the two or three songs we would sing together on rare occasions, and we have repeated it for the Danes in Copenhagen and for the American Swedes in places like Rockford, Illinois, and Minneapolis, Minnesota.

Elsie Ahlwen, composer of this lovely tune, came to America from Sweden and studied at the Moody Bible Institute. After graduation she began to work among the Swedish immigrants in Chicago, and later became a full-time evangelist. The words of this refrain had been known to her for a long time, and she often sang it to her own melody in evangelistic services throughout the country. It came to be the theme song of Elsie Ahlwen's ministry.

During a meeting in Chicago, Miss Ahlwen was approached by an old man who gave her the words for the stanzas. They had been written by Fred Blom, a former Christian worker in Sweden. Blom had come to New York early in the twentieth century, and, through circumstances that are not quite clear, had fallen into sin and was sent to prison. It was there, sick in soul and in body, that he found Christ anew. The song was his expression of joy because God had healed his backsliding and forgiven all his sin.

In keeping with the immigrant background of the song, it must be noted that the original was in the Swedish tongue. Not until the time of a great revival in Duluth, Minnesota, was this hymn first translated into English. "He the Pearly Gates Will Open" has now been rendered in more than a dozen languages.

Before hearing this hymn story, I had always wondered just what was behind the words of the second stanza:

> Like a dove when hunted, frightened,
> As a wounded fawn was I,
> Broken hearted, yet He healed me:
> He will heed the sinner's cry.

This was Fred Blom's experience. At one time he had known God's peace and victory over sin, but he had fallen victim to the temptations of this world. Yet the love of Christ would not let him go. It pursued him relentlessly, almost as a hunter stalks a deer, and finally the arrow of conviction brought him down. We are reminded of the words of David in Psalm 38:1–2: "*O Lord, do not rebuke me in Your wrath, nor chasten me in Your hot displeasure! For Your arrows pierce me deeply, and Your hand presses me down.*"

It is always tragic when a Christian falls into sin, because he loses his sweet fellowship with God and compromises his witness for Christ. Yet all of us have failed at one time or another. We may not have committed some grossly evil act, but we have "fallen short" in word or thought or deed. Perhaps we have failed to do some deed of kindness, or to show love and concern for others. How wonderful to know that God "is married to the backslider" (cf. Jeremiah 3:14). He will not allow us to be comfortable in our failure. Still His love follows us—sometimes it is shown in trouble and affliction—until we come to our senses and return to Him.

The hymn's message is very simple. Because of the love of God expressed in Christ, our sins are forgiven, our lives are changed, and we anticipate a joyful entrance into heaven. It is said that Fred Blom died in the custody of the law. While the gates of prison did not open for him, he knew that heaven's "pearly gates" would be swung wide by his Redeemer.

Elsie Ahlwen's personal testimony voices the same assurance. She had married Daniel A. Sundeen, a businessman, and they had continued a ministry together while raising their family. In 1962, they visited Chicago once again and sang "Pearly Gates" for their many friends. Shortly after, Mr. Sundeen took sick and died within a week. Mrs. Sundeen wrote these words: "It is difficult to see beyond the bend in the road where your loved one disappeared. But how good it is to know that, when my Lord calls me, the Pearl Gates will open—not because of my worthiness but because He purchased my salvation."

Prayer for the Day:

I am grateful that You, Lord, forgive me when I fall short in word or thought or deed. Thank You for loving me enough to pursue me until I return to You. Keep me from failing You and sustain me with Your love throughout my whole life.

Trusting Jesus

Edgar Page Stites, 1876

Ira David Sankey, 19th c.

1. Sim - ply trust - ing ev - ery day, trust - ing through a
2. Bright - ly doth His Spir - it shine in - to this poor
3. Sing - ing if my way is clear, pray - ing if the
4. Trust - ing Him while life shall last, trust - ing Him till

storm - y way; e - ven when my faith is small,
heart of mine; while He leads I can - not fall,
path be drear; if in dan - ger, for Him call,
earth be past; till with - in the jas - per wall,

Refrain

trust - ing Je - sus, that is all.
trust - ing Je - sus, that is all.
trust - ing Je - sus, that is all. Trust - ing as the
trust - ing Je - sus, that is all.

mo - ments fly, trust - ing as the days go by;

2

trust-ing Him what-e'er be-fall, trust-ing Je - sus, that is all.

Trusting Jesus
Hymn story by Billy Graham

"Trusting Jesus" is a hymn that is completely American in background. Edgar Stites, author of the words, was a direct descendant of John Howland, one of the *Mayflower*'s passengers. Active in the Civil War, he was later a riverboat pilot and then a missionary to the frontier churches in South Dakota.

The hymn poem first appeared in a newspaper and was handed to the American evangelist D.L. Moody. In turn, Moody gave it to his soloist and song leader, Ira D. Sankey, asking him to set it to music. In his book *Sankey's Story of the Gospel Hymns*, the singer says, "I assented, on condition that he should vouch for the doctrine taught in the verses, and he said he would."

This hymn was the favorite of my longtime friend Dr. W.B. Riley, and it expresses well the motivating purpose of his life. During the more than forty years that Dr. Riley was the beloved pastor of the First Baptist Church in Minneapolis, Minnesota, he was a pillar of strength in the evangelical movement. He appeared many times at the Florida Bible Institute while I was a student there. He—and others like Dr. H.H. Savage, Dr. William Evans, and Dr. Vance Havner—instilled in me a love for the Word of God and gave me my first doctrinal anchorage.

The frequent theme of Dr. Riley's preaching was the grace of God. He both taught and lived a practical Christianity that is proclaimed in this motto and title: "Trusting Jesus, That Is All."

I have often emphasized that becoming a Christian is more than making a decision to live a better life or to attend church more regularly. When by faith we accept Christ as our Lord and Savior, something supernatural takes place. He comes to dwell in our hearts, and gives us His own supernatural life—eternal life.

But it would be a mistake to imagine that from then on, we are automatically and almost magically victorious over sin and doubt. Not so! Each day we must have the same trust we experienced when we first came to know Christ. We all remember the words in Ephesians 2:8, "*For by grace you have been saved through faith.*" But too many people forget Hebrews 10:38, "*Now the just shall* live *by faith.*" This is the secret of living the Christian life—everyday faith—"simply trusting every day."

Each day we renew our faith in God's forgiveness. Sometimes after years of walking with God, the devil will tempt us to doubt our salvation.

But on the strength of God's Word, we can exercise faith and trust and drive the sin of doubt away.

We "simply trust" that God will keep us, guide us, and protect us each day. It is probably a good thing that we "*do not know what a day may bring forth*" (Proverbs 27:1). For if we were to see the road ahead for the next month, or year, or ten years, we would probably not have the courage to face it.

The author Robert Louis Stevenson once said, "Every man can win through until nightfall." The Christian would agree, "Yes—with the consciousness that I am God's and He is mine!" God has not promised strength or grace or faith for tomorrow. He has said, "Your strength will equal your days" (cf. Deuteronomy 33:25).

If we use our resources of prayer, of God's Word, and of Christian fellowship—and if we exercise faith and trust for each day—we can live daily in glorious victory!

Prayer for the Day:

Because of the promises in Your Word, dear God, I know that You will give me victory over sin and doubt. Today I renew my faith in Your forgiveness and trust You to guide me and protect me as I follow You.

O That Will Be Glory for Me

Charles Hutchinson Gabriel, 1900   Charles Hutchinson Gabriel, 1900

1. When all my la-bors and tri-als are o'er, and I am safe on that
2. When, by the gift of His in-fi-nite grace, I am ac-cord-ed in
3. Friends will be there I have loved long a-go; joy like a riv-er a-

beau-ti-ful shore, just to be near the dear Lord I a-dore
heav-en a place, just to be there and to look on His face
round me will flow. Yet, just a smile from my Sav-ior, I know,

will through the a-ges be glo-ry for me.
will through the a-ges be glo-ry for me.
will through the a-ges be glo-ry for me.

Refrain

O that will be glo-ry for me, glo-ry for me,
O that will be glo-ry for me, glo-ry for

glo-ry for me!   When by His grace I shall look on His face,
me,   glo-ry for me!

that will be glo - ry, be glo - ry for me!

O That Will Be Glory for Me
Hymn story by Cliff Barrows

It is often difficult to predict whether or not a new hymn will "catch on" with the public. Actually, only a small number of those that are published ever reach a second edition. Of the 6,500 hymns written by Charles Wesley during the eighteenth century, probably no more than two hundred are sung anywhere today. The *Methodist Hymnal* (1964), compiled by Americans of the Wesleyan tradition, contained only seventy-nine of Charles Wesley's hymns. Even so, this is a remarkable record of poetic longevity that is not equaled by any other hymnwriter.

When "O That Will Be Glory for Me" first appeared in 1900, a musical expert predicted, "It will never go. It has too many quarter notes." In other words, "the rhythm is too monotonous." But in a few years, it was the most popular hymn Homer Rodeheaver led in the Billy Sunday campaigns. It was affectionately called the "Glory Song" and was inspired, not by an experience, but by a personality!

The author, C.H. Gabriel, was perhaps the best known and most prolific Gospel songwriter of the early twentieth century. One of his good friends was Ed Card, superintendent of the Sunshine Rescue Mission of St. Louis, Missouri. Ed was a radiant believer who always seemed to be bubbling over with Christian joy. During a sermon or a prayer he would often explode with "Glory!" just as some people say "Amen!" or "Hallelujah!" His beaming smile earned him the nickname "Old Glory Face." It was his custom to close his fervent prayers with a reference to heaven, usually ending with the phrase "and that will be glory for me!"

No doubt many Christians have a false view of what heaven will be. Our critics often say that we yearn for "pie in the sky, by and by," while failing to really confront the issues that face us here and now. It is true that heaven will be free of the sorrow and death, the pressures and conflicts which overwhelm us on earth. But it is not a truly Christian motive to look for heaven simply because we will have no problems there.

Many folks have a similar misconception of what the Bible calls eternal life, imagining that this is the life which begins when we die or when Christ returns to this earth. "Eternal" life means a new *quality* of life—a supernatural life which begins when we enter God's family. The Bible says it clearly: *"And this is what God has testified: He has given us eternal life, and this life is in his Son. Whoever has the Son has life; whoever does not have God's Son does not have life"* (1 John 5:11–12, NLT). We believe that heaven is really a continuation of that eternal life which we may possess right now.

At the same time, one of the delightful prospects of eternity is that we will be able to accomplish the things which are, for one reason or another, impossible in this world. For one thing, we will have new bodies which will not be limited by time or space. We believe also that many of the "mysteries of our faith"—mysteries because of our mental limitations—will then be made clear. We expect that we will gain victory over all our doubts and over the sinful weaknesses which plague us now. Some people contend that it is possible that we will continue to grow mentally and spiritually through all eternity. Furthermore, it is reasonable to anticipate that in heaven God will have service for us to perform, although the Bible does not specifically list our responsibilities.

I have heard some people say that they expect to be musical experts in heaven, although they have little musical talent now. It is true that we will all be able to sing the anthem mentioned in Revelation 5:12: "*Worthy is the Lamb who was slaughtered—to receive power and riches and wisdom and strength and honor and glory and blessing*" (NLT).

What this "Glory Song" really says is that the central attraction in heaven will be Jesus Christ. We will see Him then face to face, not "*imperfectly, like puzzling reflections in a mirror*" (1 Corinthians 13:12, NLT). And all the changes that will take place in us will happen because "*when He is revealed, we shall be like Him, for we shall see Him as He is*" (1 John 3:2).

> I shall see Him, I shall be like Him,
> By one glance of His face transformed;
> And this body of sin and darkness
> To the image of Christ conformed. (A.J. Gordon)

Prayer for the Day:

Dear God, I look forward to the day when I will see You face to face. In the meantime, help me to live each day in communion with You, sharing with others the joy and eternal life available to anyone who believes in Jesus Christ.

I Will Sing of My Redeemer

Philip Paul Bliss, 1876   James McGranahan, 1877

1. I will sing of my Re-deem-er and His won - drous love to me;
2. I will tell the won-drous sto - ry, how my lost es - tate to save;
3. I will praise my dear Re-deem-er, His tri - um - phant power I'll tell,
4. I will sing of my Re-deem-er, and His heaven - ly love to me;

on the cru - el cross He suf - fered from the curse to set me free.
in His bound-less love and mer - cy, He the ran - som free-ly gave.
how the vic - to - ry He giv - eth o - ver sin and death and hell.
He from death to life hath brought me, Son of God, with Him to be.

Refrain

Sing, O sing of my Re-deem - er,
Sing, O sing of my Re-deem-er, sing, O sing of my Re-deem-er,

with His blood He pur-chased me;
with His blood He pur-chased me, with His blood He pur-chased me;

on   the cross   He sealed my par - don,
on   the cross He sealed my par-don, on   the cross He sealed my par-don,

paid   the debt   and made me free.
paid   the debt and made me free, and made me free, and made me free.

I Will Sing of My Redeemer
Hymn story by Cliff Barrows

More than one hundred years of worldwide popularity have established the Gospel song "I Will Sing of My Redeemer" as part of our musical heritage. Less well known, however, is the miraculous legend of how it was preserved for the future. The composition was found in a piece of baggage rescued from a fiery train wreck on December 20, 1876. The poem's author, thirty-eight-year-old Philip P. Bliss, had been traveling with his wife to Chicago for an engagement at D.L. Moody's Tabernacle. Near Ashtabula, Ohio, a bridge collapsed and the train plunged into an icy river bed. It is said that Bliss survived the fall and climbed out through a coach window only to return, looking for his wife. Reunited, they died together in the flaming wreckage.

These circumstances, to all appearances, cut a brilliant career short, very suddenly. It had only been two years that Bliss had served as soloist and song leader in the evangelistic campaigns of Major D.W. Whittle. All his life, it would seem, had been leading up toward this ministry. Born in a log cabin, young Philip had left home at the age of eleven to work on farms and in lumber camps. He had become a Christian at the age of twelve and soon afterward developed interest in studying music.

In the early nineteenth century, popular music training in America was centered in "singing schools"—schools which were characterized by a strong spiritual emphasis and which also provided social activity for small towns and rural communities. The singing school was strictly a one-person operation; a musician with some degree of ability traveled from place to place, organizing the classes, teaching them, and collecting his fees (which might be paid either in cash or in farm produce!).

Most of the classes in sight reading and in conducting were held at night. In the country schoolhouses, churches, or town halls, the students sang the syllables (do-re-mi) while seated on planks placed between two chairs. Each music student also "beat time" for himself by moving his hand and arm in a prescribed pattern. Many of our early Gospel musicians started out as singing school teachers. This tradition lasted more than a hundred years and had a profound effect on the quality of congregational singing and the development of church choirs.

Philip Bliss found himself strongly attracted to singing school life. At the age of 21, he married and a year later began a career as an itinerant music teacher. Using a little twenty-dollar folding organ hauled from place to place by his faithful horse, Fanny, he taught music during the winter. During the summer he became a student himself at the Normal Academy of Music at Geneseo, New York.

Song writing came naturally to Bliss; he composed equally well in both words and music. Even during his short lifetime he was recognized as the leading writer of simple sacred songs. The *Baptist Hymnal* published in 1956 included twelve hymns for which Bliss wrote either the words or the music, or both.

Although Bliss's ministry was very brief, his influence has continued down through the years. It was D.L. Moody who challenged him to leave teaching and to give his time to evangelistic Crusades. In turn, Bliss urged his close friend and fellow musician James McGranahan to undertake similar Gospel work. It was McGranahan who took Bliss's place in that weekend meeting at the Moody Tabernacle in Chicago, after Bliss died en route. Later, McGranahan joined the evangelistic party of D.W. Whittle.

We team musicians have been greatly inspired by the lives and contributions of these early evangelistic song leaders. And today—more than a century later—God still uses their simple songs and hymns to touch people's hearts, and to challenge many to decide for Christ.

God may not give each of us a great talent to use for Him. We may not have many years of service. But what we have in talent and in time is enough for God to bless and to use in accomplishing His purposes.

This song by Philip Bliss is a very simple expression of the truth of the Gospel—so obvious that it does not require elaboration. In fact, the title itself might be considered the motto of his short and brilliant life: "I Will Sing of My Redeemer."

Prayer for the Day:

Jesus, my heart's desire is to tell others of Your wonderful love. Help me to make the most of the years I have to serve You. Take whatever talents and time You have given me and use them to accomplish Your purposes in and through my life.

All Creatures of Our God and King

St. Francis of Assisi, ca. 1225; based on Psalm 148;
tr. William Henry Draper, 1919

from *Geistliche Kirchengesäng*, 1623;
harm. Ralph Vaughan Williams, 1906

1. All crea-tures of our God and King, lift up your voice and with us sing, Al-le-lu - ia! Al-le-lu - ia! Thou burn-ing sun with gold - en beam, thou sil - ver moon with soft - er gleam:
2. Thou rush-ing wind that art so strong, ye clouds that sail in heaven a - long, O praise Him, Al-le - lu - ia! Thou ris-ing morn, in praise re-joice; ye lights of eve - ning, find a voice!
3. Thou flow-ing wa - ter, pure and clear, make mu - sic for thy Lord to hear, Al-le-lu - ia! Al-le - lu - ia! Thou fire so mas-ter-ful and bright, that giv - est us both warmth and light:
4. All ye who are of ten-der heart, for - giv-ing oth-ers, take your part. Al-le-lu - ia! Al-le - lu - ia! Ye who long pain and sor - row bear, praise God and on Him cast your care!
5. And Thou, most kind and gen-tle death, wait - ing to hush our lat-est breath, O praise Him, Al-le - lu - ia! Thou lead - est home the child of God, and Christ our Lord the way hath trod:
6. Let all things their Cre - a - tor bless and wor-ship Him in hum-ble-ness! O praise Him, Al-le - lu - ia! Praise, praise the Fa -ther, praise the Son, and praise the Spir - it, Three in One:

O praise Him, O praise Him! Al - le - lu - ia!

Al - le - lu - ia! Al - le - lu - - ia!

All Creatures of Our God and King
Hymn story by Tedd Smith

One of my favorite hymn tunes, and one that I often play in sacred concerts, is associated with what has been called "Nature's Hymn of Praise"—namely, "All Creatures of Our God and King." It was written by Francis of Assisi, one of the most interesting figures in all church history. The melody is of unknown origin but was first published in a hymnal in 1623.

Francis was born into the carefree life of a wealthy Italian family in 1182. At an early age he was converted to Jesus Christ. Renouncing his life of ease, he became an itinerant evangelist who roamed through the countryside, working with the peasants and preaching to them. He gathered about him a large group of followers with whom he toured the Mediterranean lands for fourteen years. The message he proclaimed was that love for Christ leads to a life of sacrifice and of brotherly love.

This "patron saint of animals" came to love God's world of nature, probably because he lived a simple life so close to it. His hymn expresses the truth that all creation praises its Creator. It may have been based on Psalm 145:10–11: "*All Your works shall praise You, O Lord. ... They shall speak of the glory of Your kingdom, and talk of Your power.*"

The hymn is similar in form to the *Benedicite*, a traditional church canticle which is taken from the Septuagint version of the Scriptures. The *Benedicite* calls upon "showers and dew," "frost and cold," "lightnings and clouds," as well as "green things" and "fowls of the air" to "bless the Lord." It begins with the words: "O all ye works of the Lord, bless ye the Lord; praise him and magnify him forever."

All earth's creatures derive life from God and depend on Him for the continuance of their existence. Inferior animals are not capable of knowing the Almighty, yet the Bible says that they "wait upon God" because they seek their food according to natural instinct. "*That You may give them their food in due season. ... You open Your hand, they are filled with good,*" explains Psalm 104:27–28.

It is said that Saint Francis wrote these words during the hot summer of 1225 when he was very ill and losing his sight. To add to his discomfort, a swarm of field mice were trying to take over his little straw hut. No doubt he encouraged even the mice to praise God!

O all ye Beasts and Cattle, bless ye the Lord! (*Benedicite*)

It is not difficult to see that the cosmic universe shows the power and glory of God. As Psalm 97:6 says, *"The heavens declare His righteousness, and all the peoples see His glory."*

In our day, the telescope reveals much about space that was not known before. We are told that if our sun were hollow, it could hold more than a million worlds the size of our earth. But some of the remote stars are so vast that they could hold half a billion of our suns! There are about 100 billion stars in the average galaxy, and at least 100 million galaxies in known space. And many scientists believe that we have probed only one billionth of "theoretical space"!

O ye Sun and Moon, bless ye the Lord.
O ye Stars of Heaven, bless ye the Lord.

The microscope reveals that ours is a God of *little* things, as well. The ocean is teeming with tiny living forms called plankton. One variety of plankton is the diatom, a form of life related to seaweed. The diatom is so small that it would take 15 million to fill a thimble, yet each one is a marvel of beautiful and intricate design. Like the snowflakes, it seems that no two are alike!

O ye Whales, and all that move in the Waters: bless ye the Lord.

And what of man, the crowning achievement of the creative acts of God? Is not human personality the outstanding marvel in a world of wonders? God has lavished more love and care on man than on all the rest of His world. Jesus said, *"Are not two sparrows sold for a copper coin? And not one of them falls to the ground apart from your Father's will. ... Do not fear therefore; you are of more value than many sparrows"* (Matthew 10:29–31).

Unlike the rest of God's creation, we have been given a soul and spirit with which we may know our Creator. We can praise God in a way that is denied the rest of the universe—by responding to the love of God with our entire being!

O ye Children of Men, bless ye the Lord.
O ye holy and humble Men of heart, bless ye the Lord. Praise him, and magnify him for ever!

Prayer for the Day:

Your world, dear God, displays Your power and wonder. Even as I care for Your creation, I want to respond to You with my life. I love You and desire to reflect Your love in all that I do.

Once for All

Philip Paul Bliss, 1873

Philip Paul Bliss, 1873

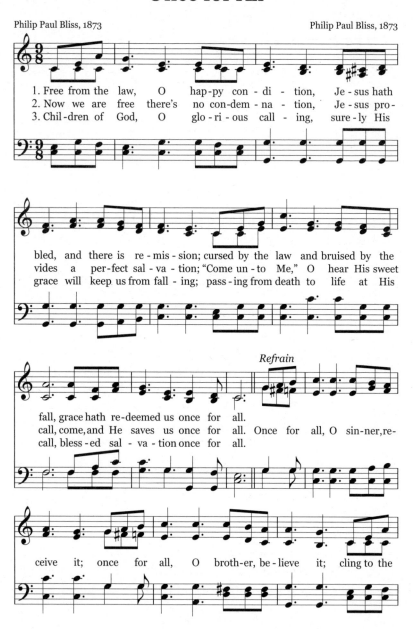

1. Free from the law, O hap-py con - di - tion, Je - sus hath
2. Now we are free there's no con-dem - na - tion, Je - sus pro -
3. Chil-dren of God, O glo - ri - ous call - ing, sure - ly His

bled, and there is re - mis - sion; cursed by the law and bruised by the
vides a per-fect sal - va - tion; "Come un - to Me," O hear His sweet
grace will keep us from fall - ing; pass-ing from death to life at His

Refrain

fall, grace hath re-deemed us once for all.
call, come, and He saves us once for all. Once for all, O sin-ner, recall, bless - ed sal - va - tion once for all.

ceive it; once for all, O broth-er, be - lieve it; cling to the

cross, the bur-den will fall, Christ hath re-deemed us once for all.

Once for All

Hymn story by Billy Graham

While we were ministering in Edinburgh, Scotland, in 1955, our Association was able to give some financial assistance to the famous Carrubbers Close Mission, which was founded by D.L. Moody many years earlier. In appreciation, the mission leaders helped us acquire the reed organ which had been used by the Gospel singer Ira D. Sankey when he and Moody worked together in Great Britain. The little organ was preserved and exhibited in our offices in Minneapolis, Minnesota, for many years.

Every time I saw it there, I was reminded of Sankey's first appearance in Edinburgh. The Presbyterians in Scotland had long insisted that only the psalms should be sung in church, and these without any accompaniment. On an earlier occasion, one lady had walked out on a Moody-Sankey meeting because of Sankey's organ, protesting that the devil was in his "kist [chest] o' whistles." Sankey's concern about the Scots' acceptance of his simple Gospel hymns was increased when he saw the great preacher and hymn writer Horatius Bonar in the audience. As he recounted it in *My Life and the Story of the Gospel Hymns*, this is what happened:

> Of all men in Scotland he was the one concerning whose decision I was most solicitous. He was, indeed, my ideal hymn writer, the prince among hymnists of his day and generation. And yet he would not sing one of his beautiful hymns in his own congregation ... because he ministered to a church that believed in the use of the Psalms only.

> With fear and trembling I announced as a solo the song, 'Free from the Law, oh, happy condition.' ... Feeling that the singing might prove only an entertainment and not a spiritual blessing, I requested the whole congregation to join me in a word of prayer, asking God to bless the truth about to be sung. In the prayer my anxiety was relieved. Believing and rejoicing in the glorious truth contained in the song, I sang it through to the end.

> At the close of Mr. Moody's address, Dr. Bonar turned toward me with a smile on his venerable face, and reaching out his hand he said: "Well, Mr. Sankey, you sang the gospel tonight." And thus the way was opened for the mission of sacred song in Scotland.

The choice of song Ira Sankey made that night had truly been dictated by God's leading. Its statement of faith included the whole story of sin and death, of grace and salvation. What better appeal could be made to a people who prided themselves on their doctrinal scholarship!

This simple hymn contains the basis of our Christian theology, from the fall of man to his final redemption in heaven. The Bible says that the devil, in the form of a serpent, tempted the first man and caused him to sin, to fall from his state of perfect fellowship with God. Genesis 3:15 teaches that Satan "*bruised the heel*" of man in this act. When the created being thus became estranged from his Creator, determined to work out his own destiny, God gave a set of laws to show that people cannot please Him in their own strength; neither can we find complete happiness in ourselves or in our relationships with others.

The penalty for breaking God's law is death, as stated in Romans 6:23: "*For the wages of sin is death.*" Furthermore, God knew that nobody could keep the law perfectly; this failure must ultimately pass a death sentence on the entire human race. This universal judgment is confirmed in Galatians 3:10: "*Cursed is everyone who does not continue to do everything written in the Book of the Law*" (NIV).

In His great wisdom and because of His great love, God provided that His Son Jesus Christ would bear our penalty and make possible the restoration of fellowship. Now we are "*free from the law of sin and death*" (Romans 8:2). Galatians 3:13 says that "*Christ has redeemed us from the curse of the law.*"

The title of this hymn comes from Hebrews 10:10, "*By that will we have been sanctified [set apart, made holy] through the offering of the body of Jesus Christ once for all.*" Jesus died on Calvary almost two thousand years ago, but His death provides salvation for all who have believed in Him, and for all who will believe in the years to come.

When we accept Christ's sacrifice for us, there is "no more condemnation." God forgives all our sins, and by so doing, frees our consciences from a sense of guilt. The Bible testifies that then "*the Spirit Himself bears witness with our spirit that we are children of God*" (Romans 8:16). We have "*passed from death into life*" (John 5:24). In addition, we are given the promise that Christ will keep us from falling into sin again if we walk day by day as His Word teaches us. "*Now to Him who is able to keep you from stumbling, and to present you faultless before the presence of His glory with exceeding joy, to God our Savior, who alone is wise, be glory and majesty, dominion and power, both now and forever. Amen*" (Jude 1:24–25).

All this information is contained in the Gospel song "Once for All." This hymn is more than a century old, but its message is timeless. It is just as relevant today as the Scriptures upon which it is based.

Prayer for the Day:

God, I am grateful for Your timeless message of salvation for all people. My faith in Your Son's death and resurrection enables me to approach Your throne in humility and freedom. Work through my life to let others know of this Good News.

I With Thee Would Begin

Karolina Wilhelmina Sandell-Berg, ca. 1875
translated Axel Samuel Wallgren, alt.

Wilhelm Theodor Söderberg, 1884,

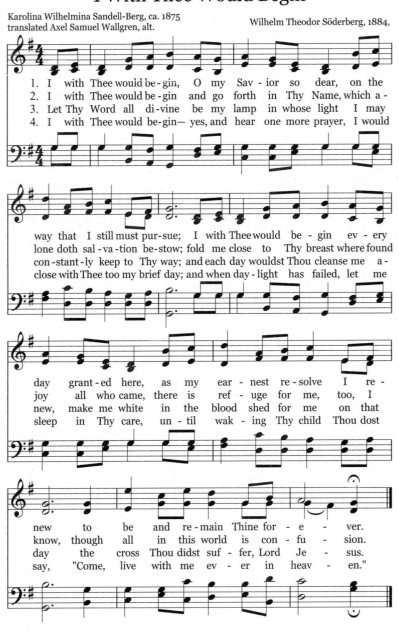

1. I with Thee would be-gin, O my Sav-ior so dear, on the
way that I still must pur-sue; I with Thee would be-gin ev-ery
day grant-ed here, as my ear-nest re-solve I renew to be and re-main Thine for - e - ver.

2. I with Thee would be-gin and go forth in Thy Name, which a-
lone doth sal-va-tion be-stow; fold me close to Thy breast where found
joy all who came, there is ref - uge for me, too, I
know, though all in this world is con - fu - sion.

3. Let Thy Word all di-vine be my lamp in whose light I may
con-stant-ly keep to Thy way; and each day wouldst Thou cleanse me a-
new, make me white in the blood shed for me on that
day the cross Thou didst suf - fer, Lord Je - sus.

4. I with Thee would be-gin— yes, and hear one more prayer, I would
close with Thee too my brief day; and when day-light has failed, let me
sleep in Thy care, un - til wak - ing Thy child Thou dost
say, "Come, live with me ev - er in heav - en."

I With Thee Would Begin

Hymn story by Cliff Barrows

What a wonderful thing it is to be able to begin again! What if, having made a bad start in a subject in school or with a project at work, we were doomed to receive a failing grade or to be dismissed from our job? How much more tragic life would be if we could never recover from the bad starts we all make in moral and spiritual ways. In his poem "Birches," Robert Frost says: "I'd like to get away from earth awhile / And then come back to it and begin over." The first part of his wish will never be realized; but we can all stay right where we are and begin over again.

This is one of the benefits that salvation brings. We can forget our old sins and failures because God has forgotten them. Through the Prophet Jeremiah, God has said, "*I will forgive their wickedness, and I will never again remember their sins*" (Jeremiah 31:34, NLT). The Bible talks about "books" (Daniel 7:10; Revelation 20:12) and suggests that all our shortcomings are recorded from the day of our birth. But when we accept Christ's offer of forgiveness, our embarrassing and condemning record is blotted out. In a past generation they would have said, "The slate was wiped clean."

More than this, we are given a completely new nature—the nature of God—so that we need not be dominated by our weaknesses as we were before. Second Corinthians 5:17 says: "*This means that anyone who belongs to Christ has become a new person. The old life is gone; a new life has begun!*" (NLT).

Of course, we continue to make occasional bad starts throughout life. Even after Christ dwells within us, we may be tempted to err and spoil our record. But Christians too can begin again. First John 1:7, 9 says: "*If we really are living in the same light in which he eternally exists, then we have true fellowship with each other, and the blood which his Son shed for us keeps us clean from all sin. ... If we freely admit that we have sinned, we find God utterly reliable and straightforward—he forgives our sins and makes us thoroughly clean from all that is evil*" (Phillips). Remember that John is writing here to Christians, to those who "*are living in the light of God's presence*" (v. 7, NLT).

Sometimes we hear the idea mentioned that, after a certain age, a person cannot change. It is true that our patterns of behavior are pretty well established when we are young. But it is also true that a person can change and be changed at any age, with the help of God. At any time in life, we can win victory over an attitude or a habit, and we can begin again. The Apostle

Paul was probably thinking of some old failures of his own when he said, near the end of his life: *"Forgetting the past and looking forward to what lies ahead, I press on to reach the end of the race"* (Philippians 3:13–14, NLT).

Some folks talk about "turning over a new leaf" at the beginning of a new year. Others seem to be cynical about New Year's resolutions because they are often forgotten by the 5th of January. When this happens, it is either because we did not really mean to keep them or because we tried to do so in our own human strength. Only God can give us the power to change and to be changed.

Each morning is a good time to begin again. In our period of personal worship, we can ask God for strength and grace to live that day in victory, accomplishing all that we would like to do. And, if we find that we have failed by noon, even then we can begin again.

In its original form, this is a Swedish hymn whose author is unknown. Because the translation is literal, you may find that the sentence structure is occasionally inverted and the meaning is a bit obscure. But if you make the effort to understand, you will find that it is a prayer that we may start anew right now in the strength of Christ and with guidance from His Word. And if you take the trouble to sing it, you will enjoy its "Swedish style" melody.

Prayer for the Day:

Lord, help me to live each day, in Your strength, with guidance from Your Word. Thank You for giving me a new start when I received You as my Savior, and remind me that I can begin again even when I stumble.

Lord, I Have Shut the Door

William M. Runyan, 1923   William M. Runyan, 1923

1. Lord, I have shut the door, speak now the word
2. Lord, I have shut the door, here do I bow;
3. In this blest qui - et - ness clam - or - ings cease;
4. Lord, I have shut the door, strength - en my heart;

which in the din and throng could not be heard;
speak, for my soul at - tent turns to Thee now.
here in Thy pre - sence dwells in - fi - nite peace;
yon - der a - waits the task— I share a part.

hushed now my in - ner heart, whis - per Thy will,
Re - buke Thou what is vain, coun - sel my soul,
yon - der, the strife and cry, yon - der, the sin:
On - ly through grace be - stowed may I be true;

while I have come a - part, while all is still.
Thy ho - ly will re - veal, my will con - trol.
Lord, I have shut the door, Thou art with - in!
here, while a - lone with Thee, my strength re - new.

Lord, I Have Shut the Door
Hymn story by Don Hustad

> *"When you pray, don't be like the hypocrites who love to pray publicly on street corners and in the synagogues where everyone can see them. I tell you the truth, that is all the reward they will ever get. But when you pray, go away by yourself, shut the door behind you, and pray to your Father in private. Then your Father, who sees everything, will reward you."* (Matthew 6:5–6, NLT)

Here's a good question to ask ourselves. Are we ever guilty of praying horizontally—for people, instead of vertically—to God? When we lead in prayer at home or in church, are we too concerned about the impression we are making on other people? Well, even if we do not indulge in "show off" prayer, this is still good advice: "When you pray, go away by yourself, all alone."

I must admit that this can be very difficult to do. From the moment a day begins, life is a bustle of activity: getting the children off to school, answering the telephone, rushing to the airport, going to meetings or to our own church, entertaining our friends, and keeping up with music practice and correspondence.

Even on the rare occasions when families are at home today, they are seldom really quiet. The noise of traffic, of jet airplanes, of telephone and television, of music and radios, bores in upon them. Someone has said that the hearing capacity as well as the spiritual tone of the present generation is bound to be harmed by the "high decibel" rate of life as we know it.

It may be that modern people don't really want to be quiet, because then they are forced into sober and serious thinking. We hide from our inner fears, our weaknesses and failures, by constant talking and doing. If we commit some sin—if one says an unkind word or thinks an evil thought—we shut it out of our mind by rushing to some new task or to another chat on the telephone. We need often to "shut the door" and pray, in order that we might really know ourselves and understand our deepest problems.

It is also true that unless we pray in this manner prescribed by our Lord, we do not really find God! Do you remember the story of Elijah's flight from King Ahab and Queen Jezebel? He was on the mountain called Horeb waiting to hear from God. First Kings 19:11–12 says that:

> *a great and strong wind tore into the mountains and broke the rocks in pieces before the Lord, but the Lord was not in the wind; and after*

the wind an earthquake, but the Lord was not in the earthquake;
and after the earthquake a fire, but the Lord was not in the fire; and
after the fire a still small voice.

God is not going to shout at us over the noise and the busy-ness of our lives. His voice is a quiet one, but it can be heard if we follow the psalmist's advice: "*Be still, and know that I am God*" (Psalm 46:10).

Every individual must solve for himself this problem of securing privacy so that he can think and pray. It may be that in your home, only the basement is out of the main stream of traffic. My wife complains that the children are always bursting in with some problem about clothes or dates, even into the bedroom at night. Some people find they can pray best in the early morning, before the telephone, radio, and TV get into gear. Others can do it while riding the train or bus to work. (If you obey the command "watch and pray" in an ultra-literal sense, you may also commune with God while you're driving.) You can even pray while walking your dog late in the evening! However you or I work it out, every one of us needs to shut the door on our busy world if we are to really pray.

William M. Runyan, author of both words and music of this hymn, was the kind of person who had evidently learned this secret. I remember him as a charming, friendly man of great dignity who occasionally dropped in at the Moody Bible Institute while he was editing hymnals for the Hope Publishing Company. Earlier in life he had been a Methodist pastor and evangelist.

Our last visit together was during his retirement in Galveston, Texas, when the Moody Chorale sang there. His very manner and his conversation revealed that, although he knew much about the world in which he lived, his greater acquaintance with God had given him a serenity which is rare in these hectic days. The dynamic for personal poise and power in meeting life's problems is found in these words of Scripture: "Go away by yourself, all alone, and shut the door behind you and pray to your Father secretly, and your Father, who knows your secrets, will reward you" (cf. Matthew 6:6).

Prayer for the Day:

Dear Father, show me ways to find those quiet times and places when I can be alone with You. Reveal to me those sins that interfere with my relationship with You, and give me the strength to turn from that sin. Whisper Your will to my heart, and give me ears to hear.

Satisfied

Clara Tear Williams, 1875

Ralph Erskine Hudson, 1875

1. All my life-long I had pant-ed for a drink from some cool spring,
2. Feed-ing on the husks a-round me till my strength was al-most gone,
3. Poor I was, and sought for rich-es, some-thing that would sat-is-fy,
4. Well of wa-ter, ev-er spring-ing, bread of life so rich and free,

that I hoped would quench the burn-ing of the thirst I felt with-in.
longed my soul for some-thing bet-ter, on-ly still to hun-ger on.
but the dust I gath-ered round me on-ly mocked my soul's sad cry.
un-told wealth that nev-er fail-eth, my Re-deem-er is to me.

Refrain

Hal-le-lu-jah! I have found Him Whom my soul so long has craved!

Je-sus sat-is-fies my long-ings, through His blood I now am saved.

Satisfied

Hymn story by George Beverly Shea

When I was a boy of eight, our family moved from Winchester, Ontario, to Houghton, New York. My father had been a pastor in Winchester for twenty years and was now beginning a brief period of ministry in evangelism and church pioneering.

Walking together in Houghton one day, Dad pointed out a tall, elderly lady moving slowly along the sidewalk. He told me that she was Mrs. Clara Tear Williams, a much loved and respected hymn writer—author of one of his favorite Christian songs, "Satisfied." From that time on, Mrs. Williams' appearance always reminded me of the classic painting of Whistler's mother. She had a regal and dignified bearing, and yet she had the kindness and gentleness of Christ in her face. When I came to know her and often spoke with her, I enjoyed the soft, musical tones of her voice. Through her sweetness and graciousness to everyone, she became another wonderful proof to me of the reality of the Christian walk. Hers was a beautiful life not only exhibited to the whole community, but also expressed in the pages of hymnals.

Some time afterward I memorized this hymn. It became one of my first solos as I began to sing publicly in my late teens. At that time my father had a pastorate in Ottawa, Canada. Since then I have always loved to sing it, because "All my life-long" expresses the conviction of everyone who has found satisfaction in Jesus Christ.

Like my family, Mrs. Williams was a Wesleyan Methodist. The composer of the hymn's melody, Ralph E. Hudson, was associated with the older Methodist Episcopal Church. After serving as a male nurse during the Civil War, he became a music teacher and publisher in Ohio. He was often engaged as an evangelistic singer and wrote many Gospel hymn tunes.

Clara Williams' hymn is as modern as the concerns of humankind. Psychologists refer to a person's fundamental needs—a need for security, a need to be loved, and a need to find identity. In this hymn these inner longings are represented by metaphors of hunger, thirst, and a desire for material riches. Many men and women pursue these elemental physical wants, thinking that they will meet their deeper needs. But, of course, they never do.

Others expect that happiness will result from gratifying the desires of the mind and the ego. A thirst for knowledge and a hunger for power characterize many people, accompanied by a desire for status and recognition. But these ambitions, too, finally become futile; as the hymn says, they are only dust which we gather around us.

King Solomon exemplified a person who relentlessly pursued satisfaction in many areas. As a young man, he enjoyed everything that could please the body: rich foods, exotic wines, and other sensual pleasures.

When he became king of Israel, Solomon experienced great power and glory. He was a connoisseur of the arts and built one of the world's most beautiful temples. He displayed great wisdom in his judgments and even practiced religion, but without true faith in God.

At the end of life, Solomon looked back over his long and fruitless quest for happiness and exclaimed, "Vanity, vanity, all is vanity!"

The final stanza of the hymn says that Jesus Christ alone can meet our deepest longings. He becomes to us a "well of water," the "bread of life," and "untold wealth that never faileth." Recall these words spoken by Jesus Himself:

> *If anyone thirsts, let him come to Me and drink.* (John 7:37)

> *I am the bread of life. He who comes to Me shall never hunger, and he who believes in Me shall never thirst.* (John 6:35)

> *Seek first the kingdom of God and His righteousness, and all these things shall be added to you.* (Matthew 6:33)

The truth is, no one can ever find true happiness apart from Jesus Christ. As St. Augustine said in his prayer long ago, "Thou hast created us for thyself, and our heart cannot be quieted till it may find repose in thee."

Prayer for the Day:

Dear Jesus, I am grateful that You have saved me through the shedding of Your blood. You satisfy my deepest longings and quiet my heart as I rest in You. Guide me throughout my life so that I always seek You and Your righteousness first.

We Lift Our Voice Rejoicing

Jack W. Hayford, 1960　　　　　　　　　　　　　　Jack W. Hayford, 1960

1. We lift our voice re-joic-ing, be-cause the Lord a-bove
2. We lift our eyes in faith to the cross where-on He died,
3. We lift our hearts to wor-ship the con-quering Sav-ior's name,

hath sent His son to save us, and man-i-fest His love
re-deemed at match-less price, now in Christ we're just-i-fied.
our tongues speak forth the prais-es of Him who is the same.

Let ev-ery hill re-ech-o with this the song we raise,
His blood hath washed our gar-ments, His peace hath filled our soul,
Christ Je-sus reigns in pow-er through-out e-ter-ni-ty,

"To Him whose blood hath bought us be glo-ry, power, and praise."
the cross is now our glo-ry since grace hath made us whole.
as yes-ter-day, so now, and for-ev-er He shall be.

We praise Thee, O Fa - ther, un - speak - a - ble our joy, in Christ our hearts find glo - ry sin's power can not de - stroy.

We Lift Our Voice Rejoicing
Hymn story by Cliff Barrows

"Sing unto the Lord a new song" is a challenge often repeated in the Scriptures. This means that we should not be satisfied with yesterday's Christian experiences. Each new day should bring a better understanding of God and a growing relationship with Christ. And our daily spiritual victories should be expressed in fresh words of testimony and prayer, and also in new songs of faith and worship.

To encourage the writing and singing of new hymns, in 1961 the Billy Graham Evangelistic Association conducted a "new hymn contest" together with the National Church Music Fellowship. The winning title chosen from over nine hundred entries was "We Lift Our Voice Rejoicing" written by the Rev. Jack W. Hayford, at that time a youth leader and later founding pastor of The Church On the Way in Van Nuys, California. The following is Mr. Hayford's own story of how this song was written:

> We had just concluded a conference held in the splendor of the autumn-spangled hills near Estes Park, Colorado, in 1960. The grand old hymn "To God Be the Glory" had themed the series there, and returning to Los Angeles I would hum that melody and nostalgically meditate on the beauty and blessing found during those days in the Rockies. Yet as excellent as that praiseful song is, something within me yearned to give vent to a personal expression of worship.
>
> One evening, as I left the office for home, the song came to me. Completely without labored premeditation, sparked by a glimpse of the clear, wind-driven sky which served as a backdrop to a single tree being stripped of its leaves, the words poured forth, together with the melody of the first two lines: "We lift our voice, rejoicing, because the Lord above hath sent His Son to save us and manifest His love." I turned the corner, and was confronted by the mountains north of the city. Walking briskly I added the next words: "Let every hill re-echo to this the song we raise;" then the [paraphrased] words of the ransomed multitude in Revelation, chapter five, came to mind—"To Him whose blood hath brought us be glory, power and praise."
>
> It was as though the autumn atmosphere had served as a catalyst to unleash the joy of the Lord in my soul. God's own natural

creation provided the setting, and His new creative work in me produced the song. Arriving home I went immediately to my study, and within minutes the hymn was completed. The overflow of my heart was on the paper before me.

A rich satisfaction came as I completed the song. It was the fulfillment sensed when you are able to express the emotion of a given moment; in this case, a moment when my heart thrilled at the wonder of God's creative power and the grandeur of His saving grace. For my part, at least, the hymn became a means by which I could sing to myself the praise of the living God.

Many Christians share in similar moments of spiritual exaltation when their whole being is in harmony with God the Creator. Few there are, however, that are able to capture the sensitivity of such an experience in song or the written word. Perhaps the expression of our own hymn of praise in a uniquely personal manner is limited to private devotions.

On the other hand, some Christians may develop their techniques in the use of language and melody to the point where God can use them extensively. Such a person is the author of this hymn, Jack Hayford. He recalls the time when he heard the late Phil Kerr tell the stories of famous hymns and their writers. Then fourteen years old, Hayford thought: "How wonderful! Though these men and women have long since died, their ministry still continues. How I would love to write something that would outlive me, that would be sung throughout the world by the people of God." Mr. Hayford's desire has been granted through hundreds of fine songs that he has written, including the well-known "Majesty."

Whether we write a hymn or simply join God's people in singing it, our lives and our lips should bring a new offering of praise to our Lord each day.

Prayer for the Day:

Father, You give me many reasons to rejoice—in Your creation, in the people I love, in the abilities You have given me, and most of all, in Your salvation. Forgive me when I take these blessings for granted, and give me a new praise-offering each day.

Children of the Heavenly Father

Karolina Wilhelmina Sandell-Berg, 1855;
tr. Ernest William Olson, 1925

traditional Swedish melody,
from *The Hymnal*, arr. Oskar Ahnfelt, 1925

1. Chil-dren of the heaven-ly Fa-ther, safe-ly in His bos-om gath-er;
2. God His own doth tend and nour-ish; in His ho-ly courts they flour-ish.
3. Nei-ther life nor death shall ev-er from the Lord His chil-dren sev-er;
4. Though He giv-eth or He tak-eth, God His chil-dren ne'er for-sak-eth;

nest-ling bird nor star in heav-en such a ref-uge e'er was giv-en.
From all e-vil things He spares them; in His might-y arms He bears them.
un-to them His grace He show-eth, and their sor-rows all He know-eth.
His the lov-ing pur-pose sole-ly to pre-serve them pure and ho-ly.

Children of the Heavenly Father
Hymn story by Don Hustad

Throughout the early history of the Christian church, most hymn writers were men: pastors, theologians, monks, bishops, and missionaries. But in the nineteenth century, women began to make important contributions to our hymnals. In Great Britain, there were Cecil Frances Alexander and Frances Ridley Havergal; in America, Harriet Beecher Stowe and Fanny J. Crosby; and in Sweden, Lina Sandell, the author of "Children of the Heavenly Father."

Her full name was actually Karolina Wilhelmina Sandell, and she was born in a Lutheran parsonage in 1832. In childhood she was probably known as "daddy's girl." She was not strong physically and often stayed in her father's study while her classmates were playing outdoors.

Lina's poetic gift showed itself at a very early age. When she was just thirteen, her first book of poems was published. This little volume contained some of her best-loved songs. During her lifetime she wrote 650 hymns in all, and 150 of these have been used by the church. "Children of the Heavenly Father" is perhaps the best known. When we took a choir on tour in Scandinavia years ago, our singers painstakingly learned the phonetic sounds so we could sing it in Swedish, "Tryggare kan ingen vara."

It does not take long to see that the hymn's basic message is about God's relationship as a Father to us, His children. Many of these phrases are taken almost word-for-word from the Bible. See if you can identify them as you sing the hymn or read the words.

The Bible tells us: "*What is the price of two sparrows—one copper coin? But not a single sparrow can fall to the ground without your Father knowing it*" (Matthew 10:29, NLT). Scientists tell us that it is impossible to see all the stars in our universe, even with their most powerful telescopes. Yet Psalm 147:4 says that our heavenly Father "*counts the number of the stars; He calls them all by name.*" And God cares more for us than He does for stars and sparrows!

Perhaps the hymn reminds you of these Scripture passages as well:

> *He will feed His flock like a shepherd; He will gather the lambs with His arm, and carry them in His bosom, and gently lead those who are with young.* (Isaiah 40:11)

> *For I am persuaded that neither death nor life, nor angels nor principalities nor powers, nor things present nor things to come,*

nor height nor depth, nor any other created thing, shall be able to separate us from the love of God which is in Christ Jesus our Lord." (Romans 8:38–39)

The Lord gave, and the Lord has taken away; blessed be the name of the Lord. (Job 1:21)

These stanzas come directly out of the personal experience of Lina Sandell. When she was twenty-six, while taking a boat trip with her father, he fell overboard, and she saw him drown. When she lost her earthly father, she learned even more personally the extent of the heavenly Father's love and care.

Some theologians have said that we should not think and talk so much of God as a father—that we should grow up and stand on our own two feet, instead of running to God every time we're in a little trouble.

Yet Jesus said in Luke 18:17, "*Whoever does not receive the kingdom of God as a little child will by no means enter it.*" And throughout life, as mature men and women, we should remain not childish but childlike in our faith and trust, as well as in our obedience to God.

If we do, we can say with confidence: "*We know that God causes everything to work together for the good of those who love God and are called according to his purpose for them*" (Romans 8:28, NLT).

Prayer for the Day:

Knowing that You are my heavenly Father, God, gives me confidence for each day. No matter what happens, You carry me in Your loving arms. Teach me to trust and obey You with childlike faith.

For the Beauty of the Earth

Folliott Sandford Pierpoint, 1864, alt.

Conrad Kocher, 1838;
arr. William Henry Monk, 1865

1. For the beau-ty of the earth, for the glo-ry
2. For the beau-ty of each hour of the day and
3. For the joy of hu-man love, broth-er, sis-ter,
4. For each per-fect gift of Thine, to the world so
5. For Thy Church, that ev-er-more lift-eth ho-ly

of the skies, for the love which from our birth
of the night, hill and vale, and tree and flower,
par-ent, child, friends on earth and friends a-bove,
free-ly given, grac-es hu-man and di-vine,
hands a-bove, of-fering up on ev-ery shore

Refrain

o-ver and a-round us lies;
sun and moon, and stars of light;
for all gen-tle thoughts and mild; Lord of All, to
flowers of earth and buds of heaven;
Her pure sac-ri-fice of love;

Thee we raise this our hymn of grate-ful praise.

For the Beauty of the Earth
Hymn story by Don Hustad

Suppose you were to visit a great artist in his studio, and all around you the walls were covered by his paintings. Is it possible that you might ignore all the beauty that he had created and never once mention it?

Some of us treat God's artistry this way! Our heavenly Father is the Creator and Giver of all that is beautiful in the universe. The first chapter of Genesis tells us that God approved of all His handiwork, repeating several times "and God saw that it was good." Undoubtedly He is pleased when we recognize the beauty of our world and thank Him for it. Yes, a Christian does have an obligation with regard to beauty. "*Whatever things are true, whatever things are noble ... just ... pure ... lovely ... of good report ... meditate on these things*" (Philippians 4:8).

There are many other aspects of our world which we take for granted: health, homes, friends, our country, even life itself. The hymn "For the Beauty of the Earth" lists some of God's blessings for which we may seem to be ungrateful. Do we feel that these are "secular" aspects of life and that we should limit our praying and singing to "spiritual" things? Yet all of these so-called ordinary things are the gifts of God. We should thank Him for them!

The late Dr. A.W. Tozer once said that every artist's work is in a sense "praise of God." The painter, the sculptor, and the musician are simply imitating God's own magnificent creative acts, using the talents which God has given them. For this reason, the Christian also sees the hand of God in all good art.

Not only did God put beautiful sounds and sights in the world—He also gave us ears and eyes to take them in, and minds to interpret what we hear see. It is proper to thank God for a clear mind and the joy we find in developing it through study or in research. This too is His great gift to us, and our gratitude is expressed in a stanza which is not always included in hymnals:

> For the joy of ear and eye,
> For the heart and mind's delight,
> For the mystic harmony
> Linking sense to sound and sight:
> Lord of all, to Thee we raise
> This our hymn of grateful praise.

In the remaining stanzas, author Folliott S. Pierpoint gives thanks for all human relationships, whether of family or of friends, and for the fellowship of the Christian church encircling the world. A final verse, omitted in most books, gives thanks for God Himself, who has given us all the joys and beauty of life—but more than all this, "His only begotten Son."

> For Thyself, best Gift Divine!
> To our race so freely given;
> For that great, great love of Thine,
> Peace on earth, and joy in heaven:
> Lord of all, to Thee we raise
> This our hymn of grateful praise.

When this hymn was first sung, the final phrase was:

> Christ, our God, to Thee we raise
> This our sacrifice of praise.

Perhaps the present version sings better, but it omits an important truth about church music. Throughout the Bible, singing is often spoken of as a "sacrifice"—a "sacrifice of joy" or a "sacrifice of praise." Hebrews 13:15 states this challenge: *Therefore by him [Jesus Christ] let us continually offer the sacrifice of praise to God, that is, the fruit of our lips, giving thanks to His name.*

God wants nothing more than our praise, our worship. A sacrifice is something which costs the giver a great deal. I have often encouraged song leaders and ministers of music to challenge Christian believers to really exert themselves, both physically and mentally, when they sing. One of Charles Wesley's hymns wishes for a "thousand tongues to sing my great Redeemer's praise." We should at least use the one we have, to full advantage!

"What shall I render to the Lord for all His benefits toward me? ... I will offer ... the sacrifice of thanksgiving, and will call upon the name of the Lord" (Psalm 116:12, 17).

Prayer for the Day:

Lord, I praise and worship You with my whole being, simply for who You are. Most of all, I thank You for giving me the gift of Your salvation. Out of gratitude, I want to live my life, through the power of Your Holy Spirit, to please You alone.

Steps to Peace With God

1. God's Purpose: Peace and Life

God loves you and wants you to experience peace and life—abundant and eternal.

The Bible Says ...

"We have peace with God through our Lord Jesus Christ." *Romans 5:1, NIV*

"For God so loved the world that He gave His only begotten Son, that whoever believes in Him should not perish but have everlasting life." *John 3:16, NKJV*

"I have come that they may have life, and that they may have it more abundantly." *John 10:10, NKJV*

Since God planned for us to have peace and the abundant life right now, why are most people not having this experience?

2. Our Problem: Separation From God

God created us in His own image to have an abundant life. He did not make us as robots to automatically love and obey Him, but gave us a will and a freedom of choice.

We chose to disobey God and go our own willful way. We still make this choice today. This results in separation from God.

The Bible Says ...

"For all have sinned and fall short of the glory of God." *Romans 3:23, NIV*

"For the wages of sin is death, but the gift of God is eternal life in Christ Jesus our Lord." *Romans 6:23, NIV*

Our choice results in separation from God.

People (Sinful)   God (Holy)

Our Attempts

Through the ages, individuals have tried in many ways to bridge this gap ... without success ...

The Bible Says ...

"There is a way that appears to be right, but in the end it leads to death."
Proverbs 14:12, NIV

"But your iniquities have separated you from your God; and your sins have hidden His face from you, so that He will not hear."
Isaiah 59:2, NKJV

There is only one remedy for this problem of separation.

3. God's Remedy: The Cross

Jesus Christ is the only answer to this problem. He died on the cross and rose from the grave, paying the penalty for our sin and bridging the gap between God and people.

The Bible Says ...

"For there is one God and one mediator between God and mankind, the man Christ Jesus."
1 Timothy 2:5, NIV

"For Christ also suffered once for sins, the just for the unjust, that He might bring us to God."
1 Peter 3:18, NKJV

"But God demonstrates His own love toward us, in that while we were still sinners, Christ died for us." *Romans 5:8, NKJV*

God has provided the only way ... we must make the choice ...

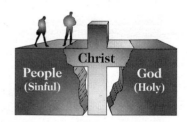

4. Our Response: Receive Christ

We must trust Jesus Christ and receive Him by personal invitation.

The Bible Says ...

"Behold, I stand at the door and knock. If anyone hears My voice and opens the door, I will come in to him and dine with him, and he with Me." *Revelation 3:20, NKJV*

"But as many as received Him, to them He gave the right to become children of God, to those who believe in His name." *John 1:12, NKJV*

"If you confess with your mouth the Lord Jesus and believe in your heart that God has raised Him from the dead, you will be saved." *Romans 10:9, NKJV*

Are you here ... or here?

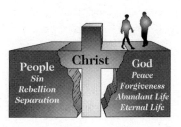

Is there any good reason why you cannot receive Jesus Christ right now?

How to Receive Christ:

1. Admit your need (say, "I am a sinner").
2. Be willing to turn from your sins (repent) and ask for God's forgiveness.
3. Believe that Jesus Christ died for you on the cross and rose from the grave.
4. Through prayer, invite Jesus Christ to come in and control your life through the Holy Spirit (receive Jesus as Lord and Savior).

What to Pray:

Dear Lord Jesus,
    I know that I am a sinner, and I ask for Your forgiveness. I believe You died for my sins and rose from the dead. I turn from my sins and invite You to come into my heart and life. I want to trust and follow You as my Lord and Savior.

                    In Your Name, amen.

_____   _____
Date   Signature

GOD'S ASSURANCE: HIS WORD

IF YOU PRAYED THIS PRAYER,

THE BIBLE SAYS ...

"For, 'Everyone who calls on the name of the Lord will be saved.'"
Romans 10:13, NIV

Did you sincerely ask Jesus Christ to come into your life? Where is He right now? What has He given you?

"For it is by grace you have been saved, through faith—and this not from yourselves, it is the gift of God—not by works, so that no one can boast."
Ephesians 2:8–9, NIV

THE BIBLE SAYS ...

"He who has the Son has life; he who does not have the Son of God does not have life. These things I have written to you who believe in the name of the Son of God, that you may know that you have eternal life, and that you may continue to believe in the name of the Son of God."
1 John 5:12–13, NKJV

Receiving Christ, we are born into God's family through the supernatural work of the Holy Spirit who indwells every believer. This is called regeneration or the "new birth."

This is just the beginning of a wonderful new life in Christ. To deepen this relationship you should:

1. Read your Bible every day to know Christ better.
2. Talk to God in prayer every day.
3. Tell others about Christ.
4. Worship, fellowship, and serve with other Christians in a church where Christ is preached.
5. As Christ's representative in a needy world, demonstrate your new life by your love and concern for others.

God bless you as you do.

Billy Graham

If you want further help in the decision you have made, write to:
Billy Graham Evangelistic Association
1 Billy Graham Parkway, Charlotte, NC 28201-0001

1-877-2GRAHAM (1-877-247-2426)

COME AWAY ...

Come away to the Blue Ridge Mountains in Asheville, North Carolina, and hear God speak through inspiring teachers, soul-stirring worship, and the breathtaking beauty of His creation.

For a free program guide, call 1-800-950-2092 or visit **TheCove.org**.

BILLY GRAHAM
Training Center *at* The Cove
A ministry of Billy Graham Evangelistic Association

©2012 BGEA